PRACTICE
MAKES
PERFECT

Spanish
Irregular Verbs
Up Close

Spanish Irregular Verbs
Up Close

Eric W. Vogt, Ph.D.

New York   Chicago   San Francisco   Lisbon   London   Madrid   Mexico City
Milan   New Delhi   San Juan   Seoul   Singapore   Sydney   Toronto

1 2 3 4 5 6 7 8 9 10 11 12 13 14 15 16   WFR/WFR   1 9 8 7 6 5 4 3 2 1 0

ISBN   978-0-07-171808-0
MHID   0-07-171808-7

Library of Congress Control Number: 2010924601

Interior design by Village Bookworks, Inc.
Interior illustrations by Glyph International

McGraw-Hill books are available at special quantity discounts to use as premiums and sales promotions or for use in corporate training programs. To contact a representative, please e-mail us at bulksales@mcgraw-hill.com.

This book is printed on acid-free paper.

Amandae, filiae carissimae meae, qui plus quam scivit semper amata est.

Contents

The Spanish verb system

·1·

An overview

When you try to conjugate Spanish verbs, do you feel as if everything you've ever been taught seems tangled in your mind like a bird's nest of fishing line at the bottom of a row boat? Does your teacher circle the verbs on your quizzes and tests, or write question marks that seem to say *where on earth did you come up with this form*? If you find yourself in a quagmire of confusion or committing the same errors time and again, using this book systematically will "reprogram" your understanding of the verb system.

This book is less concerned with the uses of the tenses and moods of Spanish verbs than with their morphology, or forms. The book focuses on irregular verbs, which of course, means that we will have to contrast them with regular verbs along the way. So, take heart. You're not alone as an intermediate student of Spanish. Jumbled verb forms are one of the things Spanish teachers see all the time in their second-year Spanish classes. Why? Because first-year students are exposed to the whole verb system, but receive little specific attention to help them step back in order to discover, recognize, and assimilate the patterns. It also takes longer than a one-year course to internalize verb patterns.

The approach used in this book is based on the fact that Spanish evolved from Latin, which is still taught using the "principal parts": four forms needed to understand the morphology of Latin's even more elaborate verb system. Although textbooks and reference works sometimes show these principal parts, they are not arranged or explained in a useful way. In Appendix A you will find a verb chart named TurboVerb. It resurrects the system of principle parts and adapts it so that it works for learning Spanish verbs. Consult TurboVerb often as you progress through each chapter in order to become familiar with it. By visualizing the morphological patterns in a new way, the fog will clear, and your tangled notions will unravel. Here is this book's promise: if you internalize and apply the information about the formation of verbs found in TurboVerb, you will be able to derive the exact form of any verb, in any tense, mood, person, and number. Just imagine how good that will make you feel! The beauty and secret of this method is that by learning only six forms of any verb, along with a handful of morphological rules belonging respectively to each of the four microsystems, you will be able to derive any form of that verb.

Begin by visualizing the Spanish verb system as a system of systems. Ready? *Imagine four boxes inside one big box.* This arrangement represents how the Spanish verb system can be broken down into four microsystems, each one represented by its own box.

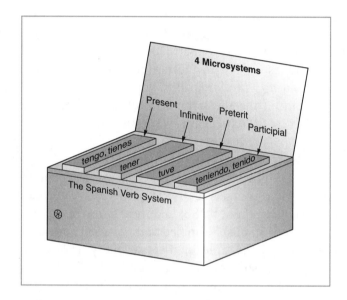

Each microsystem has rules for deriving only a couple of tenses apiece, thus cutting the problems down to size. That should reduce your anxieties considerably since, as you know from frustrating experience, some verbs are regular in all their forms in all tenses and moods, while others are irregular only in one of the microsystems, and still others are irregular in all forms except their infinitives. But, as this book unpacks the systems and you learn six forms of each verb you know or acquire along the way, you will have all you need to derive any and all forms of every verb. As is to be expected, there are some verbs that don't work perfectly with this method, but fortunately they are few: **dar, estar, haber, ir, saber,** and **ser.** But even these verbs have some patterns that parallel other verbs.

The six forms of any verb that you need to know in order to master this system are: (1) the first- and (2) second-persons singular of the present indicative; (3) the infinitive; (4) the first-person singular of the preterit indicative; and the two participles— (5) the gerund and (6) the past, or passive, participle. In order to reinforce the essential notion that the Spanish verb system is a macrosystem consisting of four microsystems, these forms should be separated by semicolons as shown by the following example of **tener**, a high-frequency and quite irregular verb. Note how the systems, when written in list form, are separated with commas and semicolons:

tengo, tienes; tener; tuve; teniendo, tenido

Now refer to the TurboVerb chart. There, you'll see that **tener** is the verb selected as a model for this principal parts method for learning Spanish verbs. As you relearn the verb system, pay close attention to how you should visualize the six forms you have to learn and how to write them on lists of verbs to learn, as modeled here.

The *first two* forms (the first- and second-persons singular: **tengo** and **tienes**) belong to the first of the four microsystems, which I have dubbed the *present system*. Since these first two forms of the six you must memorize belong to the same microsystem, they are separated by commas, then followed by a semicolon to set them off as members of the present system. The *third* form of any verb you need to memorize is the infinitive (**tener**). As the form itself suggests, I've named this second microsystem the *infinitive* system. The *fourth* form is the first-person singular of the preterit indicative (**tuve**) and the third system is called the *preterit* system. Finally, the *fifth and sixth* verb forms together comprise the *participial* system. The *fifth* form (**teniendo**) is called the *present participle*, which, depending on its use, is also referred to as the *gerund*. Finally, separated by a comma from the fifth form, the *sixth* form to be learned (**tenido**) is the *past participle*, also called the *passive participle*, for reasons that will be explained in Chapters 10–12.

Notice that this method does not have you conjugating by starting with the infinitive every time you need to derive the right person, number, tense, and mood of a verb. You almost certainly have learned your verbs by starting from their infinitives. It is likely that you also have difficulty recalling an infinitive when you see or hear a conjugated verb form. Attempting to derive the form you need by beginning from an infinitive causes most of your problems and frustrations with Spanish verbs. When you converse or read in the real world, you most often encounter conjugated forms rather than infinitives, so you aren't supplied with the necessary information for deriving the form you need at the moment. Knowing only the infinitive tells you nothing about whether or not the verb is irregular, or how and in which tenses and moods it is irregular. With the method in this book, you begin learning the verbs as vocabulary items with six forms each, the first two being from the present indicative. The infinitive, important as it is as a reference point, turns out to be morphologically less important, so it comes third.

As you apply the rules pertaining to each of the four microsystems represented by the four boxes, any form of every verb in the Spanish language can appear as if by magic in the boxes any time you think of that verb and the six forms you have memorized for it. When you use your imagination to open the box labeled *present*, you will see two forms, and from one of them derive the form in the person and number you need. In the second box, a small one labeled *infinitive*, you will see one form and derive from it the person and number of that verb in one of the three tenses derived directly from the infinitive. Likewise, in the third box, even though it is a large one, you will see one word, from which you will be able to derive the person and number of one of the two tenses and moods of the *preterit* system. In the last box, one of the two small ones, you'll see two words that are invariable in form and are used to form *progressives*, *passive* voice constructions, and the seven *perfect* tenses, as can be seen in TurboVerb.

Since intermediate students have been exposed to all the tenses and moods, and since this book is about clearing up confusion about their forms and uses, your first task, after doing the morphology exercise at the end of this chapter, is to go to any list of infinitives you have or wish to create and rewrite it in this format. As you do the exercise at the end of this chapter, you will probably relive the frustration that comes from having learned to reference verbs from the infinitive and then slowly pick your way through the tenses in the order in which you learned them, by person and number. But as you look up the forms you need to fill in the blanks, you will see that the principal parts method used in this book is the only sure way to cure your confusion. In a nutshell, this method provides you with all the patterns you need in order to know your way around the whole verb system from any form in which you happen to encounter a verb.

When you learn verbs according to this principal parts pattern and the handful of derivation rules associated with each microsystem, you will be able, at a glance, to identify the tenses in which a given verb is regular or irregular. You can find more examples in the upper right-hand portion of the second page of TurboVerb and in an additional listing of "survival verbs" included as Appendix B.

After you have looked up and listed as many verbs as you wish to tackle, your next task will be to learn the four sets of rules to apply within each microsystem in order to derive the forms of all the tenses within it. With the exception of a small group of verbs that have a simple vowel change in their stem, these derivation rules do not jump from microsystem to microsystem. These rules are the subject of each chapter in this book.

Chapter 2 begins with the present indicative and the irregular patterns found in this tense and mood. Subsequent chapters examine the tenses pertaining to each microsystem, and you'll learn the rules to apply for deriving the forms of the tenses that belong to that microsystem. The exercises that follow each chapter focus on the forms you need to master by using the principle parts system illustrated in TurboVerb, whose use is explained in detail in Appendix A. You are encouraged to write your answers to the exercises in pencil or on a separate sheet of paper, since they bear repeating.

Fill in the blanks to supply the missing forms of the six forms of the following verbs. Don't worry—you're expected to use some reference work to look these up. At this point, the goal is to internalize the pattern by knowing what form goes in each position.

1. _____ , quieres; _____ ; _____ ; queriendo, querido

2. veo, _____ ; _____ ; vi; viendo; _____

3. _____ , dices; _____ ; dije; _____ , dicho

4. abro, _____ ; abrir; abrí; abriendo, _____

5. _____ , pones; _____ ; _____ ; poniendo; _____

6. _____ , _____ ; hacer; hice; haciendo; _____

7. traigo, traes; _____ ; _____ ; _____ , traído

8. _____ , conoces; conocer; _____ ; conociendo, conocido

9. traduzco, _____ ; _____ ; _____ ; traduciendo, traducido

10. sirvo, _____ ; _____ ; serví; _____ , servido

11. hablo, _____ ; _____ ; _____ ; hablando, hablado

12. busco, _____ ; buscar; _____ ; buscando, buscado

13. vivo, vives; _____ ; viví; _____ , vivido

14. _____ , pides; _____ ; pedí; _____ , pedido

15. _____ , pierdes; _____ ; perdí; perdiendo, perdido

16. corro, _____ ; _____ ; corrí; corriendo, corrido

17. leo, _____ ; _____ ; leí; _____ , leído

18. vuelvo, _____ ; volver; volví; volviendo, _____

19. escribo, escribes; _____ ; escribí; escribiendo, _____

20. _____ , _____ ; morder; mordí; mordiendo, mordido

21. puedo, puedes; _____ ; _____ ; pudiendo, podido

22. _____ , mueres; _____ ; morí; _____ ,

_____

23. como, _____ ; comer; comí; comiendo, _____

24. rompo, _____ ; _____ ; rompí; rompiendo, _____

25. huelo, _____ ; _____ ; olí; oliendo, olido

Present system 1

Present indicative

Imagine moving from left to right in our imaginary box representing the Spanish macrosystem. The first microsystem is the box on the extreme left, labeled the *present system*. You can find that box represented by the first column in TurboVerb. Examining that column, you will discover that there are three members of the present system: the *present indicative*, the *present subjunctive*, and the *imperative* (or *command* forms). Although this chapter is dedicated to the present indicative only, all the information you need to derive any verb form in the three moods of the present system is found in this column (except, as noted in Chapter 1, for **dar**, **estar**, **haber**, **ir**, **saber**, and **ser**).

To help you navigate through future chapters, a bit of terminology is important at this point: *Tense* refers to the *time* of action—in this case, the present. In Spanish, the word for *tense* is **tiempo**, which is much more literal than the English term. For instance, a command can take place at no other time but in the present. Think of *mood* as referring to the function a verb form has—the way it is used or its mode of operation. As its name suggests, the *indicative* mood *indicates*; that is, it points out or declares information about an action. For the purposes of this chapter, this is all you need to know about the concept of mood.

Logically, if there is such a thing as an irregular verb, there must be some pattern it deviates from, something that defines what regular is. So, in order to understand irregular verbs, you have to be sure that you know what regular verbs look like. Let's review the regular pattern for **-ar**, **-er**, and **-ir** verbs in the present indicative. The traditional model verbs for these three families are **hablar**, **comer**, and **vivir** because they are regular in all tenses and moods. As we examine all the tenses throughout the book, we will start by taking a look at how these three verbs are conjugated. Let's examine the present indicative forms of these model verbs:

hablo	hablamos	como	comemos	vivo	vivimos
hablas	habláis	comes	coméis	vives	vivís
habla	hablan	come	comen	vive	viven

Next, it is important to learn some predictable patterns in this tense and mood. Compare the various personal endings in all three families of verbs. Notice that, in the present indicative, the first-person singular form (**yo**) ends in an -**o**. The first-person plural form (**nosotros** and **nosotras**) ends with the personal ending -**mos**, while the third-person plural (**ellos**, **ellas**, and **ustedes**) ends with -**n**. Note that in *all* tenses and moods the -**mos** and -**n** endings are the identifying markers for these two persons and numbers—even for irregular verbs! The endings of the other persons and numbers are not so consistent.

Now, having seen what regular verbs look like in the present indicative, we can turn our attention to the various irregular patterns in this tense and mood. One oddity is that in the present indicative of regular -**ir** verbs, the theme vowel of the infinitive, **i**, is changed to an **e**—except for the first- and second-person plurals (the **nosotros** and **vosotros** forms). This pattern gives the appearance of a *shoe* or *boot* if you enclose the remaining forms by drawing a line around them.

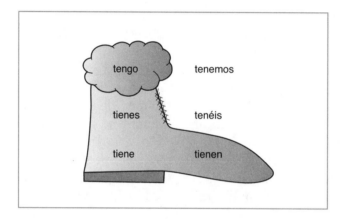

Even though we refer to the shoe or boot pattern in the context of irregular stem patterns, this particular feature is *regular* with regard to the *ending* vowels in -**ir** verbs.

It is precisely the other changes that can happen in the *stem* or *root* of the verb—the part before the -**ar**, -**er**, and -**ir**—that make verbs irregular. These are called *stem changes*. Fortunately, even the irregularities fall into patterns and groups. There are six possible ways in which verbs can be irregular in the present tense. In summary form they are:

1. Single vowel to diphthong: **o** → **ue**, in a shoe or boot pattern

2. Single vowel to diphthong: **e** → **ie**, in a shoe or boot pattern (as in the figure above)

3. Single vowel to single vowel: **e** → **i**, in a shoe or boot pattern

4. Consonant change in the first-person singular only: **c** → **zc**

5. Consonant change in the first-person singular without any vowel change in that person and number (**yo** form) *and* a single vowel to diphthong change in the remainder of the shoe or boot pattern: **g, ie**

6. Consonant change in the first-person singular *and* a single vowel to single vowel change in the remainder of the shoe or boot pattern: **g, i**

By far the most frequent irregular patterns found in the present system are when the vowel changes into a diphthong, as in Types 1 and 2 in the preceding list. Another valuable bit of information about all stem-change irregularities is that the syllable of the change is the one that is stressed, that is, it's the syllable pronounced more forcefully than the others. This fact will help you speak Spanish better, so as you examine the following present indicative examples of these high-frequency types, pay particular attention to the shoe or boot pattern:

puedo	podemos
puedes	podéis
puede	**pue**den

pienso	pensamos
piensas	pensáis
piensa	**pie**nsan

Other examples of the less numerous Type 1 irregular, but nonetheless high-frequency, verbs include **duermo, duermes (dormir)** and **muero, mueres (morir)**. They also exhibit this stem-vowel irregularity in the shoe or boot pattern. Other Type 2 verbs include **entiendo, entiendes (entender); quiero, quieres (querer);** and **miento, mientes (mentir)**.

Next, there are a handful of high-frequency Type 3 verbs, such as **sirvo, sirves (servir); pido, pides (pedir);** and **recibo, recibes (recibir)**. Once again, this stem-vowel irregularity is also found in the shoe or boot pattern. It is worth pointing out that the single vowel to single vowel irregularity is also found in the preterit system in these same verbs; however, this irregularity will not exhibit the same pattern as in the present system.

Another common irregular pattern is Type 4, when a verb shows some consonant change in the first-person singular only. The rest of the persons and numbers are regular. Some examples include verbs whose infinitives end in -ecer: **parezco, pareces (parecer)**, as well as verbs whose infinitives end in -**ucir: traduzco, traduces (traducir)** and **conduzco, conduces (conducir)**. Also in this group are many, but not all, verbs often called "g-stems," such as **salgo, sales (salir)** and **pongo, pones (poner)**. In the present indicative, this irregularity appears only in the **yo** form.

conozco	conocemos
conoces	conocéis
conoce	conocen

pongo	ponemos
pones	ponéis
pone	ponen

The verb used as a model in TurboVerb, **tengo**, **tienes** (**tener**), is an example of Type 5 of irregularity in the present system. Another common Type 5 verb is **venir**. It is a g-stem verb, but it additionally exhibits a consonant change in the first-person singular and a single vowel to diphthong change in the rest of its conjugation, following the shoe or boot pattern in the present indicative:

vengo	venimos
vienes	venís
viene	vienen

Lastly, the Type 6 pattern is found in the high-frequency verb **decir** and its compounds. Note that in the indicative mood the g-stem is found in the **yo** form of the present, and the **e → i** irregularity follows the shoe or boot pattern, as shown:

digo	decimos
dices	decís
dice	dicen

The two exercises in this chapter focus exclusively on the irregular verbs of the present indicative. The second set also adds the challenge of using other elements to construct grammatical sentences. Remember to identify the subject of each verb so that you select the correct set of endings while paying attention to the first two principal parts so that you can identify the irregular patterns.

EJERCICIO
2·1

Fill in the blanks with the proper form of the verbs in parentheses, using the present indicative. In the case of reflexives, don't forget to include the proper form of the pronoun in the blank.

1. (poder) Los niños _____ vestirse solos.

2. (ser) Tú _____ un estudiante muy talentoso.

3. (decir) Yo siempre _____ la verdad.

4. (querer) Ella _____ invitarlo a la fiesta.

5. (huir) Yo _____ de los engaños del mundo.

6. (estar) Él _____ en clase.

7. (ponerse) Yo _____ el impermeable si llueve.

8. (ir) Tú y yo _____ de compras mañana.

9. (conducir) Yo _____ con cuidado en la ciudad.

10. (saber) ¿Qué _____ yo de eso?

11. (perder) Los niños _____ la carrera.

12. (parecerse) Juana, es obvio que tú _____ a tu mamá.

13. (sentirse) Ellos _____ mal hoy por lo de ayer.

14. (sentarse) Yo _____ en esta silla, gracias.

15. (aborrecer) Yo _____ los cuentos de aparecidos.

16. (pedir) Ella nos _____ un favor.

17. (pensar) Ellos _____ que es ridículo comprar billetes de lotería.

18. (servir) Los meseros me _____ el pescado ahora.

19. (caerse) La niña _____ en la acera de vez en cuando.

20. (volar) El avión _____ a San Francisco todos los días.

25. (entender) Parece que hoy hay menos que _____ la evolución que hace veinte años.

26. (construir) En mi ciudad, hay muchos hombres que _____ rascacielos.

27. (oír) Perdóname, pero yo no _____ bien.

28. (dormir) ¿_____ tú ocho horas todos los días?

29. (hervir) El agua _____ cuando la temperatura alcanza los 100°C.

30. (traducir) Yo _____ documentos científicos todos los días.

Dehydrated sentences. *Use the following elements, making whatever additions and changes necessary, to create grammatically correct sentences in the present indicative.*

1. ella/siempre/mentir/novio

   _____

2. yo/dar/clases/inglés/extranjeros

   _____

3. ella/conducir/loca

   _____

4. yo/salir/clase/temprano

   _____

5. ellas/venir/Los Ángeles

   _____

6. yo/tener/jugar/con/hija

   _____

7. yo/poder/jugar/tenis

   _____

8. ella/venir/Colombia

   _____

9. Ud./poder/manejar/carro

   _____

10. ellos/saber/tocar/piano

    _____

11. yo/hacer/dibujos/cuaderno

    _____

12. tú/entender/discurso/político

    _____

13. nosotros/dormirse/diez/todas/noches

_____

14. yo/poner/disco

_____

15. tú/querer/estudiar/Chile

_____

16. mis hermanos/pensar/tú/tener razón

_____

17. ellos/pensar/viajar/Rapa Nui/verano

_____

18. mi amigo/saber/yo/decir/verdad

_____

19. yo/no saber/hablar/chino

_____

20. tú/querer/mudarse/Puerto Rico

_____

21. yo/saber/tú/saber/verdad

_____

22. Juan/parecerse/su hermano

_____

23. yo/conocer/su hermana

_____

24. ella/encender/luz

_____

25. Ud./ser/científico importante

_____

26. tú/traducir/documentos/contabilidad

_____

Present system 2

Present subjunctive

The forms of the *subjunctive mood* in the present tense are derived from the **yo** form of the present indicative—the first-person singular—and thus pertain to the present microsystem, the first column in TurboVerb. As its name suggests, the subjunctive is used in certain types of *sub*ordinated clauses, that is, in clauses that have been introduced by some other verb. In order to understand what the endings are for the present subjunctive, examine this tense and mood using the traditional models of regular verbs:

hable	hablemos	coma	comamos	viva	vivamos
hables	habléis	comas	comáis	vivas	viváis
hable	hablen	coma	coman	viva	vivan

Remember that in conjugating the present subjunctive the **-ar** verbs change the theme vowel that identifies their infinitive to an **e** while the **-er** and **-ir** verbs change to **a** before adding the personal endings such as **-mos**, **-s** or **-n**. This morphological feature of the present subjunctive is one more reason why learning only the infinitive form as your starting point for conjugation is not a good idea. Not only could **-ar** verbs be confused with **-er** verbs, but if you see or hear an **-er** or **-ir** verb in the present subjunctive and need to use it in some other tense and mood, you cannot tell from its present subjunctive form whether it is **-er** or **-ir**.

Another important feature of the present subjunctive is that, unlike the pattern present indicative endings, the first-person singular and third-person singular of all verbs in the present subjunctive are identical in form. This happens in other tenses as well, so it is important to become accustomed to it. One result of this is that personal pronouns tend to be needed a bit more when using the first- and third-persons singular in order to make it clear just who the subject of the verb is.

Irregularities do not impact the endings, only the stems. That is, no matter what type of irregularities are seen in the stem, for all irregular types the endings are not affected in any way—the subjunctive endings are the same as if they were regular.

However, even though the irregularities in the present subjunctive are the same irregularities you saw in the present indicative in Chapter 1, the stem changes do not always follow the shoe or boot pattern in the present subjunctive. Compare the indicative and the subjunctive of the following common irregular verbs and look at the irregular patterns listed for the present system in the left-hand column of TurboVerb. Notice that for verbs with a single vowel to diphthong change in the **yo** form—Types 1 and 2—the shoe or boot pattern of the stem *is* retained in the present subjunctive:

INDICATIVE		SUBJUNCTIVE	
puedo	podemos	pueda	podamos
puedes	podéis	puedas	podáis
puede	pueden	pueda	puedan
pienso	pensamos	piense	pensemos
piensas	pensáis	pienses	penséis
piensa	piensan	piense	piensen

In the previous chapter about the indicative forms, you learned that Type 3 verbs exhibit a shoe or boot pattern with respect to the vowel stem change of single vowel to single vowel. This pattern does not occur in the subjunctive forms of Type 3 verbs. Instead, the irregularity is seen in *all six* persons and numbers. Compare the indicative and subjunctive forms as shown here:

INDICATIVE		SUBJUNCTIVE	
sirvo	servimos	sirva	sirvamos
sirves	servís	sirvas	sirváis
sirve	sirven	sirva	sirvan

Once again, the value of this adaptation of the ancient principle parts system is obvious. How much more useful it is to learn the forms **sirvo**, **sirves** (**servir**) than to learn **servir** all by itself and then hope you can recall how this verb quite literally *morphs* in its various tenses and moods!

Next, let's take a look at the Type 4 verbs whose only change in the indicative was a consonant irregularity in their **yo** form. Into this group we also added those g-stem verbs that only had that consonant irregularity and no vowel changes in the indicative forms. Just as with Type 3 verbs, in the present subjunctive of these verbs the consonant irregularity also appears in *all six* persons and numbers, as the following contrastive examples show:

INDICATIVE		SUBJUNCTIVE	
conozco	conocemos	conozca	conozcamos
conoces	conocéis	conozcas	conozcáis
conoce	conocen	conozca	conozcan

The same holds true for Type 5 g-stem verbs, both those that have only a consonant change in the **yo** form of the indicative and those that also have a single vowel to diphthong irregularity following a shoe or boot pattern in the indicative. In their subjunctive forms, only the consonant change appears and, once again, in *all six* forms of the present subjunctive. The stem vowel remains regular and the shoe or boot pattern is lost, as this example shows:

INDICATIVE		SUBJUNCTIVE	
pongo	ponemos	ponga	pongamos
pones	ponéis	pongas	pongáis
pone	ponen	ponga	pongan
vengo	venimos	venga	vengamos
vienes	venís	vengas	vengáis
viene	vienen	venga	vengan

The Type 6 pattern is found in the high-frequency verb **decir** and its compounds. Note that in the indicative mood the g-stem is found in the **yo** form of the present and the **e → i** irregularity follows the shoe or boot pattern; yet in the subjunctive mood, *both* the **g** and the **e → i** are present in *all six* persons and numbers:

INDICATIVE		SUBJUNCTIVE	
digo	decimos	diga	digamos
dices	decís	digas	digáis
dice	dicen	diga	digan

Lastly, verbs whose infinitives end in **-car**, **-gar**, and **-zar** undergo a spelling change in the present subjunctive, which is necessary to preserve their regular pronunciation. If Spanish had no written form, they would be considered regular. Think of these verbs as sounding regular, but with a spelling change to reflect this. These changes are found in verbs whose infinitives end in **-car**, **-gar**, and **-zar**, which change to **-que**, **-gue**, and **-ce**, respectively, to preserve the consonant sound of the hard **c** or **g**. In the case of the **z**, the change is due to decree from the **Real Academia Española**, or Royal Spanish Academy. Observe the following examples:

buscar		pagar		empezar	
busque	busquemos	pague	paguemos	empiece	empecemos
busques	busquéis	pagues	paguéis	empieces	empecéis
busque	busquen	pague	paguen	empiece	empiecen

Fill in the blanks with the proper form of the verbs in parentheses, using the present subjunctive. In the case of reflexives, don't forget to include the proper form of the pronoun in the blank.

1. (querer/ver) Nosotros no _____ que tú _____ esa película.

2. (dudar/ser) Ellos _____ que ese político _____ honesto.

3. (decir/ir) Su papá le _____ a su hijo que _____ a Europa a estudiar.

4. (creer/saber) Yo no _____ que los administradores _____ lo que hacen.

5. (ir/despertarse) Nosotros _____ al parque después de que mamá

   _____ .

6. (querer/oír) ¿_____ tu papá que nosotros _____ esa ópera?

7. (insistir/ponerse) La mamá _____ en que sus hijos _____ los zapatos.

8. (alegrarse/traducir) Yo _____ de que tú _____ cartas comerciales.

9. (enfadarse/saber) Los profesores _____ de que los alumnos no _____ la materia.

10. (desear/conocer) Juan, yo _____ que _____ a mi vecino Tomás.

11. (rogar/perder) Señor Gómez, yo le _____ que no _____ el tiempo con esta propuesta.

12. (ser/ser) ¡_____ inconcebible que la propuesta _____ tan mal concebida!

13. (dar/sentirse) Me _____ pena que tú _____ mal hoy.

14. (recomendar/ir) Yo le _____ al decano que _____ a Sur América.

15. (ser/poder) ¡_____ fantástico que tú _____ acompañarme esta noche!

16. (buscar/merecer) Él _____ una novia que _____ su amor.

17. (ser/pensar) _____ necesario que los miembros del comité _____ mejor.

18. (pedir/traer) El cliente le _____ al mesero que le _____ una copa de Merlot.

19. (tener/caerse) Yo _____ miedo de que mi papá _____ en el jardín.

20. (tener/volar) Juan _____ miedo de que su hijo _____ a Nueva York.

21. (esperar/casarse) Ellas _____ que su hermana no _____ con Juan.

22. (ser/pensar) _____ magnífico que él no _____ como el decano.

23. (recomendar/perder) Yo te _____ que no _____ tiempo hablando de esto.

24. (tener/ver) Juan _____ miedo de que tú _____ a su ex-novia.

25. (buscar/entender) Nosotros _____ una secretaria que _____ bien las estadísticas.

26. (ser/construir) _____ increíble que ellos _____ un rascacielos en ese terreno.

27. (querer/estar) ¿ _____ tú que yo _____ aquí a las cuatro esta tarde?

28. (temer/huir) Juan _____ que los perros _____ al oír el disparo de la escopeta.

29. (ser/estar) _____ peligroso que los niños _____ en la cocina.

30. (dudar/haber/traducir) Yo _____ que aquí _____ nadie que _____ esto al ruso.

Dehydrated sentences. *Use the following elements, making whatever additions and changes necessary to create grammatically correct sentences. Of course, pay special attention to using the subjunctive form with the verb in each sentence that requires it.*

1. Juan/querer/yo/conducir/tienda.

   _____

2. tú/esperar/ella/no ir/playa.

   _____

3. ser dudoso/ellos/poder/cantar/noche.

   _____

4. ser necesario/tú/dormir/antes de que/volver/padre.

   _____

5. tú/desear/yo/buscar/un libro/ser interesante.

   _____

6. ellas/insistir/tú/venir/fiesta/temprano.

   _____

7. no haber nadie/comité/ser capaz.

   _____

8. gente tonta/no creer/ser importante aprender lenguas.

   _____

9. ¿no creer/tú/ella/ser traidora?

   _____

10. él/insistir/tú/empezar/tarea pronto.

    _____

11. dueño/te/buscar/para que/pagar el alquiler.

    _____

12. yo/te recomendar/leer novela.

_____

13. antes de que/tú y yo/tener clase mañana/ser necesario/tú/leer artículo.

_____

14. darme pena/te/doler/cabeza.

_____

15. Juan/querer/ella/encender/luz.

_____

16. ellos/pedir/yo/dar/dinero.

_____

17. mi amigo/insistir/nosotros/llegar temprano.

_____

18. yo/tener miedo de/hija/conducir carro.

_____

19. nosotros/esperar/ella/no traer/perro/fiesta.

_____

20. molestarme mucho/ellos/pedir/ese plato.

_____

21. gustarme/ella/darme/un beso.

_____

22. yo/esperar/tú/venir/fiesta mañana.

_____

23. tú y Juana/no querer/Juan/estar en la misma clase.

_____

24. nosotros/decir/Juan y Tomás/tener cuidado.

_____

25. ser fantástico/ellos/conocer/mi jefe/noche.

_____

26. ser importante/nosotros/estar/reunión.

_____

27. ¿querer/tú/nosotros/venir/diez/noche?

_____

28. mis padres/no creer/yo/tener problemas/económicos.

_____

29. Juan/decir/su hijo/no ir/montañas mañana.

_____

30. Nosotros/buscar/película/ser/intrigante.

_____

Present system 3

Imperatives

The *imperative* mood is the formal name for command forms—those forms that are used when one directly addresses a person, telling him, her, or them to do or not do something. In Spanish, they are called **mandatos**, a noun derived from the verb **mandar**, which means *to command* or *to send*. In English, the imperative is the same as the infinitive but without the preposition *to*:

> ***Run*** *to the store!*
> ***Give*** *me a refund!*

In Spanish, all the forms of the imperative mood are exactly the same as the subjunctive form of that person and number, except for the affirmative commands for **tú** and **vosotros**. This means that all the negative commands are in subjunctive form, *including* the negative **tú** and **vosotros** commands. Since you cannot command yourself, there is no command form for **yo**; however, as you saw in the previous chapter, in the present subjunctive, the **yo** form and the third-person singular (**él**, **ella**, and **usted**) are identical.

Learning the usage of the subjunctive is easier if you keep in mind that imperative forms, except the ones noted here, are simply one more use of the subjunctive form. To illustrate this, consider how one use of the subjunctive is as a verb form in subordinated noun clauses introduced by a main clause. The main verb in that clause is a verb of commanding, that is, telling someone to do something. Viewed this way, command forms are simply sentences with an unspoken main clause. Examine the following examples and note how they show the progression from a full sentence that shows one person's wish that someone else do something, to an indirect command, and finally to a direct command:

Statement

Voy a decirle al Sr. Pardo **que compre** el carro.	*I'm going to tell Mr. Pardo to buy the car.*

Indirect command

Que el Sr. Pardo **compre** el carro.	*Let Mr. Pardo buy the car.*

Direct command

Sr. Pardo, ¡**compre** el carro!	*Mr. Pardo, buy the car!*

Notice that the first statement is made up of two clauses: a main clause (**Voy a decirle al Sr. Pardo**) followed by **que**, the conjunction that introduces a subordinated clause (**compre el carro**). The speaker is not addressing Mr. Pardo but someone else instead.

Moreover, the subordinated clause cannot stand alone as a statement indicating a fact, not even with **que** in front of it. As a statement expressing a fact, that is, indicating, asserting or pointing out information, the form would have to be in the indicative mood: **[El Sr. Pardo] compra el carro** (*Mr. Pardo buys the car*). When **que** is used in front of the clause, Spanish speakers will understand the expression as an indirect command. Note that the English word *let* in the previous translation does not mean "allow" because it is not a command to the other listener. Finally, in direct address, the speaker turns to Mr. Pardo and uses the same form to tell him to buy the car.

In all three examples, the verb **comprar** is in the subjunctive form. In the first example, it is used in the way one normally thinks of when using the present subjunctive. In the second example, the subjunctive is used in what is known as the *jussive*—the name grammarians use to refer to indirect commands. Finally, the subjunctive form itself performs the function of a direct command in the **usted** form, which is used for formal or polite address.

Let us now examine all the affirmative commands, beginning with the affirmative **tú** and **vosotros** commands, and see how the principle parts method will give you the form you need, instantly. First, observe what endings we need for regular verbs. Here are the six principal parts of the traditional model verbs. You will need to refer to two when deriving the affirmative **tú** or **vosotros** commands of regular verbs.

> hablo, hablas; hablar; hablé; hablando, hablado
> como, comes; comer; comí; comiendo, comido
> vivo, vives; vivir; viví; viviendo, vivido

For the affirmative **tú** command, simply dropping the final **-s** of the **tú** form of the present indicative (the second of the six forms above) gives you the affirmative **tú** command. You may have learned to "borrow" the third-person singular of the indicative and, while that is correct, the rule is of limited value: you can use it confidently only if the verb is regular. The third-person singular of regular verbs is also the same as the infinitive minus the final **-r**, and so sometimes students are told to derive the regular **tú** command that way. Once again, this approach works only for regular verbs. On the other hand, the principal parts method for deriving the affirmative **tú** command works for all irregular verbs that have *only* a vowel stem change. For instance, the affirmative **tú** command of **pensar** is **piensa**—and the principal parts method will save you from making the mistake of missing that **e → ie** change.

For the affirmative **vosotros** command, refer to the infinitive (the third of the six principal parts) and change the final -**r** to a final -**d**. The stress falls on that last syllable, just as it does in the infinitive. All Spanish verbs, no matter how irregular, form their affirmative **vosotros** command in this way. If you're studying Castilian, the dialect of much of Spain, this is great news. However, this form of address is not often found in the Americas.

The affirmative **tú** commands of g-stem verbs are derived from the first of the six principal parts (the **yo** form). Drop the final syllable -**go** to derive the affirmative **tú** command of those verbs, the only exception being the affirmative **tú** command of **hacer**, which is **haz**.

Even among the handful of verbs that aren't friendly to the principal parts system (**dar, estar, haber, ir, saber,** and **ser**), the affirmative **tú** commands of **dar, estar,** and **saber** are regular: **da, está,** and **sabe**. As command forms, **está** and **sabe** are often avoided by using indirect commands or a full sentence: thus, their subjunctive forms are employed:

Quiero que **estés** aquí a la una.	*I want you to be here at one o'clock.*
Es importante que **sepas** esto.	*It's important for you to know this.*

Coincidentally, the **tú** command of the high-frequency verb **ir (ve)** is identical to the affirmative **tú** command of **ver (ve)**. So, to use the affirmative **tú** commands to say *Go and see!* one says **¡Ve y ve!** Finally, there is no affirmative **tú** command for **haber** in modern Spanish, since it is either an impersonal verb or the helping verb for the perfect tenses.

There is a command for **nosotros**, usually translated as *let's*, and both the affirmative and the negative are in the subjunctive. If a **nosotros** command involves a reflexive verb, the -**s** of the -**mos** ending is eliminated:

¡Acostémonos!	*Let's get to bed!*

Note that the **nosotros** command of the verb **ir** has two forms, one without and one with the intensifying reflexive: **vayamos** or **vámonos**. There is no appreciable difference in meaning.

If you examine how the various imperative forms, affirmative and negative, are arranged in TurboVerb, you'll see exactly how you should be arranging them in your head. Notice that after the affirmative **vosotros** command, the next form in the vertical list is the *affirmative* **tú** command and the next to the last one is the *negative* **tú** command. There are two reasons for this. First, they couldn't be more different, and so it is important to prevent associating the negative form with the affirmative, which could happen by their mere proximity. Second, and perhaps more important, all other commands are derived from the **Ud.** command, which, as we've seen, is simply the third-person singular of the present subjunctive (and identical to the first-person singular, which is why the present subjunctive is derived from the **yo** form). The affirmative and negative **vosotros** commands are also separated for the same reasons.

Looking closely at the pattern, you'll see that the only further changes involve adding or subtracting personal endings or adding **no** to the negative forms. The simple symmetry of the format itself will help you internalize the patterns in no time—provided you know the first three of the six principal parts.

Finally, it is important to review the placement rules for object pronouns when they are used with imperatives. While there are two options for where object pronouns can be placed with infinitives and gerunds, there are no options for imperatives. With affirmative commands, the object pronoun or pronouns must follow the command and be attached, and a written accent placed on the syllable that receives the stress before adding the syllable or syllables of the object pronoun or pronouns. For negative commands, pronouns are placed between the word **no** and the negative command, which is always in the subjunctive form.

In either situation, if both an indirect and a direct object pronoun are used, remember that they must stay together and that the indirect object pronoun (receiver of an action) is placed before the direct object pronoun. If a reflexive verb is used along with a direct object pronoun, the reflexive pronoun is placed before the direct object pronoun. The last example also serves to remind you that with verbs of hygiene, the articles are used instead of possessive adjectives when referring to parts of the body. Memorize these models so you can follow them when speaking or writing:

Affirmative command		Negative command	
¡Dámelo!	*Give it to me!*	¡No me lo des!	*Don't give it to me!*
¡Acuéstese temprano!	*Go to bed early!*	¡No se acueste temprano!	*Don't go to bed early!*
¡Lávenselas!	*Wash them (your hands)!*	¡No se las laven!	*Don't wash them!*

The exercises for this chapter consist solely of translations from English to Spanish, with some further instruction so as to elicit all four forms of *you*: **tú, usted, vosotros,** and **ustedes.** All noun objects should be changed to pronouns and placed in the proper position, according to the rules presented here.

Translate the following commands from English to Spanish, taking special note of additional instructions or hints as well as changing the object nouns to pronouns and placing them in the proper position. The needed verbs are in parentheses.

1. (**dar**) Give the books to him! (*speaking to your brother*)

   _____

2. (**traer**) Bring her the blouses! (*speaking to an older salesperson*)

   _____

3. (**venir**) Come to the party! (*speaking to a group of friends in Spain*)

   _____

4. (**saber**) Know this: he is honest! (*speaking to an audience in Latin America*)

   _____

5. (**soltar**) Let go of me! (*speaking to a stranger*)

   _____

6. (**caerse**) Don't fall down! (*speaking to a child*)

   _____

7. (**poner**) Put the books here! (*speaking to a friend*)

   _____

8. (**colocar**) Don't place the table here! (*speaking to two deliverymen*)

   _____

9. (**apagar**) Don't turn out the light! (*speaking to your friends, in Spain*)

   _____

10. (**encontrar**) Find the money! (*speaking to your friends, in Latin America*)

    _____

11. (**ver**) See the movie! (*speaking to your friend*)

    _____

12. (**buscar**) Don't look for the car now! (*speaking to your spouse*)

_____

13. (**tener**) Don't be afraid! (*speaking to a child*)

_____

14. (**salir**) Leave! (*speaking to a group of intruders, in Latin America*)

_____

15. (**empezar**) Start the music! (*speaking to a group, in Spain*)

_____

16. (**querer**) Don't want that! (*speaking to a friend*)

_____

17. (**pagar**) Pay the bills! (*speaking to your spouse*)

_____

18. (**ser**) Don't be dumb! (*speaking to a friend*)

_____

19. (**conducir**) Drive carefully! (*speaking to a stranger*)

_____

20. (**traducir**) Translate the document! (*speaking to a stranger*)

_____

21. (**llegar**) Arrive early! (*speaking to a boss*)

_____

22. (**sentarse**) Don't sit here! (*speaking to a group, in Latin America*)

_____

23. (**pensar**) Think first! (*speaking to a room of young children, in Latin America*)

_____

24. (**sentirse**) Don't feel bad! (*speaking to a stranger*)

_____

25. (**comenzar**) Start the race! (*speaking to a group, in Spain*)

_____

26. (**dar**) Give me the shirts! (*speaking to your brother*)

_____

27. (**devolver**) Return the pants! (*speaking to your friend*)

_____

28. (**proponer**) Don't propose that! (*speaking to a professional group*)

_____

29. (**aprobar**) Don't approve the plan! (*speaking to a professional group*)

_____

30. (**morirse**) Don't die! (*speaking to a friend*)

_____

Infinitive system 1

Imperfect indicative

In Spanish, the infinitive forms anchor the morphology of the tense and mood endings. Verbs ending in -**ar**, -**er**, and -**ir** have certain endings both unique to them or in common, according to analogous patterns. However, as we have seen, it is not enough to know the endings of verbs in all the tenses. The irregular patterns in verb *stems* are best and most efficiently revealed and remembered by the principal parts method. This will be even more apparent when we study the imperfect indicative, one of the three tenses derived directly from the *infinitive*, the third of the six principal parts. The infinitive represents the *infinitive microsystem*, found in the second column of TurboVerb.

In addition to pointing the way to the proper set of verb endings, according to whether a verb ends in -**ar**, -**er**, or -**ir**, the infinitive is the best starting point for the derivation of three tenses: the *future*, the *conditional*, and the topic of this chapter, the *imperfect indicative*. This tense is often clarified more precisely by noting that it is more properly understood as one of two aspects of one past tense, the *preterit* being the other.

This tense is a real gift because, among the thousands of verbs in the Spanish language, only three are irregular in the imperfect: **ser**, **ir**, and **ver**. Even **ver** is barely irregular; once upon a time, it was spelled **veer** and even though the infinitive became **ver**, its imperfect conjugation is analogous to those of **creer** and **leer**.

Though this is the most predictable of all tenses in the Spanish language, some features of its patterns, pronunciation, and usage can cause English speakers trouble. As you examine the conjugations of these three irregular verbs, you will notice something new—the **nosotros** and **vosotros** forms of **ser** and **ir** are stressed on their first syllable:

ser		ir		ver	
era	éramos	iba	íbamos	veía	veíamos
eras	érais	ibas	íbais	veías	veíais
era	eran	iba	iban	veía	veían

As we saw with the present subjunctive, the first- and third-persons singular are identical and, as in all tenses, we see -**s**, -**mos**, and -**n** as markers of the second-person singular, the first-person plural, and the third-person plural, respectively. Likewise, as we saw in the present subjunctive, -**er** and -**ir** verbs share one set of endings instead of each having its own. Let's now examine the regular endings with our traditional regular verbs, **hablar**, **comer**, and **vivir**:

hablar		comer		vivir	
hablaba	hablábamos	comía	comíamos	vivía	vivíamos
hablabas	hablabais	comías	comíais	vivías	vivíais
hablaba	hablaban	comía	comían	vivía	vivían

The imperfect indicative is usually the second tense learned after the present indicative, which has many stem changes, both consonant and vowel. At that point, you're also just beginning to remember whether a given verb is an -**er** or an -**ir** verb when you see or hear it in conjugated form. In passing, if you have already learned the conditional, which we'll cover in a separate chapter, it is important to notice that although the -**er** and -**ir** verbs end in forms of -**ía**, the conditional adds these endings without removing the -**ar**, -**er**, and -**ir** infinitive endings.

Due to its regularity, it's tempting to greet the imperfect with excitement, but this excitement can soon fade, since the distinction between -**er** and -**ir** is impossible when listening to or reading a conjugated form—unless you have learned the infinitives very well. One comforting fact about the regularity of the imperfect is that there are no stem changes in the imperfect indicative! The principal parts method keeps you from "infecting" the imperfect with the irregularities of the present by keeping the various tenses in their proper boxes in your mind when you wish to derive their conjugations. When the patterns of the present are set apart from those tenses derived from the next microsystem, the infinitive, the imperfect indicative becomes easy to form.

One common pitfall with the imperfect is pronouncing it correctly. The -**er** and -**ir** verbs share the same set of endings, and these endings are stressed on the **í**, not the **a**. Also, in addition to the stressed first syllables in the **nosotros** and **vosotros** forms of the three irregular verbs noted previously, the **nosotros** and **vosotros** forms of regular verbs have accent marks to show you which syllable is stressed.

Finally, the toughest thing about using the imperfect is knowing when to use it as opposed to the preterit. The imperfect is used to set the stage, describe, give background information, and talk about ongoing (incomplete) repeated or habitual action, as well as mental and physical conditions in the past. There are a couple of hard and fast rules: when telling time or discussing someone's age in the past, the imperfect is *always* used.

Mi papá **tenía** 25 años cuando nací.   *My father was 25 when I was born.*
Eran las cuatro cuando Juan salió.   *It was four o'clock when John left.*

Furthermore, since the imperfect is concerned with circumstance, it does not move a story along, and so it often is used *with* the preterit, which supplies the details about action. English translations of the imperfect are often periphrastic (a verb phrase) or can be rendered as such without changing the meaning. Study the following examples:

Mis amigos **iban** al cine...

My friends used to go to the movies . . .
My friends were going to the movies . . .
My friends would go to the movies . . .

Of all English modal verbs, *would* causes the most trouble when "translating" into Spanish. A good rule of thumb is that if you can use one of the other two translations instead of *would* and not change the meaning, then you almost certainly need the imperfect indicative. Otherwise, you may need the conditional or the imperfect subjunctive, both of which will be covered in later chapters.

Since all but three verbs in the imperfect are regular in Spanish, the fill-in-the-blank exercise for this chapter contains mostly regular verbs. The other exercise, however, requires you to change from some other tense or mood to the imperfect indicative of the same verb, in the same person and number.

EJERCICIO
5·1

Fill in the blanks with the proper form of the verbs in parentheses, using the imperfect indicative. In the case of reflexives, don't forget to include the proper form of the pronoun in the blank.

1. (ponerse) Los chicos _____ los pantalones cuando entró su mamá.

2. (ser) Simón Bolívar _____ un general importante en el Siglo XIX.

3. (decir) Como yo se lo _____ a mi amigo...

4. (mandar) En ese pueblo, las mujeres _____ .

5. (ver) En la playa la semana pasada, yo _____ muchas cosas interesantes.

6. (estar) ¿Dónde _____ tú ayer?

7. (poder) De niño, yo no _____ cruzar las calles solo.

8. (ir) Nosotros _____ a la tienda cuando se nos pinchó una llanta.

9. (manejar) Nosotros _____ desde Xalapa cuando oímos la noticia sobre el terremoto.

10. (conocer) Ella lo _____ muy bien cuando eran niños.

11. (perder) Pensé que _____ el juicio con toda la tarea que tenía.

12. (trabajar) Vosotros _____ en Málaga en aquel entonces, ¿no?

13. (faltar) ¡Lo que me _____ –perder la billetera!

14. (gustar) A esos niños no les _____ ese cuento de hadas.

15. (caerse) Mientras Juan _____ , logró agarrar una raíz y se salvó.

16. (repetir) Su mamá le _____ las mismas instrucciones a su hija cada día.

17. (creer) Hace 500 años, mucha gente _____ en muchas supersticiones.

18. (servir) Cuando ella nos _____ la limonada, se resbaló y se cayó.

19. (llamarse) ¿Cómo _____ tu bisabuelo?

20. (volar) Los atletas _____ a Chicago cuando empezó a nevar.

21. (poder) Cuando ellos eran niños, no _____ hablar bien.

22. (ver) Mientras nosotros _____ la película, mi mamá preparó las palomitas.

23. (ir) Nosotros _____ a la escuela cuando vimos el accidente.

24. (ser) _____ una noche de tormentas y teníamos mucho miedo.

25. (entender) Los alumnos no _____ nada de lo que decía el profesor.

26. (tener) Cuando yo _____ seis años, vivíamos en Texas.

27. (escuchar) Mientras ella _____ la radio, trabajaba.

28. (morirse) Mientras Thomas Jefferson _____ , _____ también John Adams.

29. (crecer) El jardín _____ más rápido el año pasado.

30. (crear) Da Vinci _____ muchas obras de arte mientras estudiaba ciencias.

Change the following conjugated verbs to the same person and number of the imperfect indicative.

1. dirías _____

2. trabajaré _____

3. conduje _____

4. vi _____

5. soy _____

6. voy _____

7. viste _____

8. crees _____

9. quieren _____

10. pierdo _____

11. encuentro _____

12. piensa _____

13. pensé _____

14. rompí _____

15. sería _____

16. iría _____

17. busqué _____

18. dormiría _____

19. comió _____

20. serviste _____

21. leí _____

22. di _____

23. vi _____

24. querrían _____

25. salieron _____

26. subimos _____

Infinitive system 2

Future

The second of the three tenses derived from the infinitive microsystem, or the third of the six principal parts, is what is known as the *simple future indicative*. In grammatical terminology, *simple* means that this tense is a one-word form. At the same time, this is a simple tense in that it is an easy conjugation to learn. In case you're wondering (and worrying!), there is a *simple future subjunctive*, but (to your relief!) it is only encountered nowadays in proverbs and legal documents. Its form is close to the *imperfect subjunctive* and will be shown, for completeness's sake, in the chapter devoted to that tense and mood.

If you're like most Spanish students, you probably learned the formula **ir** + **a** + infinitive. This corresponds neatly to the English phrase *to be going to*. . . . This structure is known by grammarians as the *periphrastic future,* that is, a verb phrase that does the same job as the simple future, but with more than one word.

The Spanish simple future corresponds to the English use of the modal verbs *will* + verb or *shall* + verb. In American English the differences between *will* and *shall* are now obsolete except in legal documents. As such, it is used as an absolute future injunction, as in the Ten Commandments, e.g., **¡No matarás!** (*Thou shalt not kill!*). When you are thinking from English into Spanish, the Spanish simple future covers all conceivable ranges in meaning and usage of these two forms of the future tense in English—plus one more use which we'll see shortly.

First, let's examine how to form the simple future in Spanish. The future is different from all but one other tense in that it is formed by adding only one set of endings to all three families of verbs. That is, the infinitive endings **-ar**, **-er**, and **-ir** are *not* removed first; there is only one set of endings for all verbs and the stress falls on the main vowel of these endings. The endings are interesting in themselves because they are the same as the present indicative of the helping verb **haber**, without the initial **h-**. In the case of the future of the **vosotros** form, **hab-** is removed. In fact, historically, this is how the simple future tense came into being. Documents and literature from around the time of Christopher Columbus show that the transition was in full swing (e.g., **amar has** for *you will love*).

haber

he	hemos
has	habéis
ha	han

This pattern helps many students remember the endings of **haber** when applied to form the simple future and when conjugating **haber** in the present to form the present perfect indicative of other verbs. Examine the conjugation of a familiar verb that is regular in the future and notice how **haber** can be heard and seen as if lurking on the end of the infinitive:

hablar

hablaré	hablar**emos**
hablarás	hablar**éis**
hablará	hablar**án**

Looking closely at these forms, you'll see that as with many tenses and moods, the first- and third-persons singular are identical and that the personal endings **-s**, **-mos** and **-n** are markers of the **tú**, **nosotros**, and the **ellos**, **ellas**, **ustedes** forms respectively, as they always are. Likewise, these endings are used with **-er** and **-ir** verbs:

comer		**vivir**	
comeré	comer**emos**	viviré	vivir**emos**
comerás	comer**éis**	vivirás	vivir**éis**
comerá	comer**án**	vivirá	vivir**án**

There are twelve verbs listed in TurboVerb whose stems are irregular when forming the simple future. Even their irregularities fall into three groups that are easy to identify. I call them *new d-stems*, *collapsed infinitives*, and just *totally irregular*. Notice that the new d-stem verbs all have an **-n-** or an **-l-** before the theme vowel of their infinitives (e.g., **poner**, **valer**), while the collapsed infinitives do not and are all **-er** verbs. Among the collapsed infinitive group, note that **poder** is not a new d-stem because it already has **-d-** in its stem. Fortunately, the list of totally irregular verbs in the future consists of only two: **hacer** (**har-**) and **decir** (**dir-**). Remember that the endings remain unchanged.

In order to remember (or at least appreciate) the new d-stem group, note that if you try to pronounce their future forms *without* inserting the **-d-**, they are harder to say. Your tongue is in a position where it is easier to add that consonant, a fact that partly explains how this form came to be. At a practical level, this may help you remember them.

There is one usage of the simple future in Spanish that the English future does *not* share. It is used to express what is called *probability in the present* and is one of the ways to express a common English verb that has no equivalent as a verb in Spanish: *wonder*. You can appreciate the use of the future in this way if you consider probability as a guessing game in which a fact *will be* found out. Consider the following examples of the use of the future as statements of probability in the present:

¿Dónde estará Juan?	*I wonder where John is.*
	Where could John be?
¿Qué estará haciendo Teresa en este momento?	*I wonder what Theresa is doing right now.*
	What could Theresa be up to just now?
¿Qué hora será?	*I wonder what time it is.*
	What time could it be?

EJERCICIO
6·1

Fill in the blanks with the proper form of the verbs in parentheses, using the simple future tense. In the case of reflexives, don't forget to include the proper form of the pronoun in the blank.

1. (poder) Su mamá no _____ asistir a la reunión mañana.

2. (hacer) ¿Qué _____ nosotros si se aprueba la propuesta?

3. (ver) Tú _____ lo que vamos a hacer.

4. (querer) ¿Quién _____ venir a esta ciudad si no hay empleo?

5. (decir) Yo se lo _____ luego.

6. (estar) ¿Dónde _____ María y Teresita?

7. (ponerse) Ellos _____ las botas después de comer.

8. (ir) ¿Con quién _____ tú a la playa este verano?

9. (conducir) Mis hermanos _____ el camión hasta San Diego.

10. (querer) Ella no _____ salir con él nunca.

11. (haber) ¿_____ alguien aquí que nos pueda ayudar a cambiar la llanta?

12. (parecerse) Creo que su bebé _____ a la mamá.

13. (sentir) Si no cambia de opinión, esta mujer lo _____ .

14. (venir) Mi papá _____ en julio.

15. (poder) Igual que tú, yo _____ ir al baile este fin de semana.

16. (pedir) Como siempre, Carlos me _____ los apuntes de clase.

17. (salir) Héctor _____ temprano del trabajo hoy.

18. (pedir) El mesero dice que Juan no _____ la torta de manzana.

19. (caerse) Las chicas que están patinando sobre el hielo _____ .

20. (volar) Lorena dice que pronto _____ a Chicago.

21. (tener) Emilio _____ problemas en sus exámenes si no estudia más.

22. (saber) ¡Tarde o temprano, todos _____ que tienes la culpa por cobarde!

23. (poner) Raúl _____ todo en orden antes de salir.

24. (poder) A mi ver, esto no _____ ser resuelto sin costarle algo.

25. (entender) Ipólito no _____ el plan.

26. (pasar) Dos chicos _____ por la tienda a solicitar fondos para una obra caritativa.

27. (ser) Oficialmente, _____ primavera después del equinoccio de marzo.

28. (ver) Roberto _____ la gloria que merece, un día.

29. (saber) Al morir, dicen algunos, todos nosotros _____ la verdad.

30. (parecerse) ¡Ella pronto _____ a la otra si sigue viéndola tan a menudo!

Dehydrated sentences. *Use the following elements, making whatever additions and changes necessary to create grammatically correct sentences using the simple future tense.*

1. Juan y Carlos/tener/semana libre pronto.

   _____

2. yo/poner/libros/estante esta tarde.

   _____

3. Teresa y Juana/no decir/verdad.

_____

4. ¿salir/tú/inmediatamente después/concierto?

_____

5. yo/querer/hablar/Rosa/este/fin/semana.

_____

6. ¿quién/poder/esquiar/mañana?

_____

7. ¿ver/Uds./película/conmigo?

_____

8. ella/hablar/con/tú/mañana.

_____

9. nosotros/mirar/programa luego.

_____

10. mi padre/salir/cuando/recuperarse.

_____

11. ¿quién/darme/regalo/fiesta?

_____

12. esto/no caber/este cajón.

_____

13. ¿a quién/mandarle/estos libros?

_____

14. ¿qué/hacer/decano?

_____

15. su madre/repetirle/instrucciones.

_____

16. yo/no servirle/nada.

_____

17. tú/ir/Europa/año que viene.

_____

18. ¿Uds./pedírselo/a Juana?

_____

19. yo/amarla/siempre.

_____

20. Ud./vivir/Costa Rica/diez años.

_____

21. ¿qué/decir/vecinos?

_____

22. ¿qué/comer/tú/esta noche?

_____

23. esta propuesta/crear/problemas.

_____

24. nueva cadena de montañas/formarse.

_____

25. ¿quién/creerlo?

_____

26. Mi mamá/no dármelo nunca.

_____

27. yo/escribírsela/luego.

_____

28. tú/leérselo/al niño.

_____

29. Juan/tenerlo/probablemente.

_____

30. ¿quién/estar/en la puerta?

_____

Infinitive system 3

Conditional

7

The *conditional* is the third of the three tenses derived from the infinitive microsystem. Strictly speaking, it is not a tense but rather a mood, because it doesn't refer to present, past, or future time.

The conditional is rendered in English as *would* + verb when the meaning of the English auxiliary verb *would* is used to express the consequence of some hypothetical or counterfactual situation. As such, it is used in tandem with the *imperfect subjunctive* (whose derivation we'll examine later), which sets up the *if* clause. The order of these two clauses is unimportant, but the use of the conditional is always to express the *consequence* of a hypothetical situation, as the following examples show:

Si yo pudiera, **iría** a México para estudiar.	*If I could, I would go to Mexico to study.*
No **saldría** de casa si lloviera como ayer.	*I wouldn't leave the house if it were were raining like it was yesterday.*

Like the future, the conditional is formed by adding only one set of endings to all three families of verbs. That is, the infinitive endings **-ar**, **-er**, and **-ir** are *not* removed first and there is only one set of endings for all verbs. The stress falls on the **-í-** of these endings. Examine the conjugation of the three traditional models of regular verbs to learn the endings:

hablar		comer		vivir	
hablaría	hablaríamos	comería	comeríamos	viviría	viviríamos
hablarías	hablaríais	comerías	comeríais	vivirías	viviríais
hablaría	hablarían	comería	comerían	viviría	vivirían

Once again, you should notice that as with many tenses and moods, the first- and third-persons singular are identical and that the personal endings **-s**, **-mos**, and **-n** are still the familiar markers of the **tú**, **nosotros**, and the **ellos**, **ellas**, **ustedes** forms.

Referring to TurboVerb, you'll see that the same twelve verbs whose stems are irregular in the future are also used to form the conditional. Once again, the irregularities fall into three groups: the *new d-stems*, *collapsed infinitives*, and the *totally irregular*. Remember that the new d-stem verbs have an **-n-** or an **-l-** before the theme vowel of their infinitives (e.g., **poner**,

valer) and the collapsed infinitives do not and are all **-er** verbs. Finally, the totally irregular conditional verbs are the same as the irregular future verbs: **hacer** (**har-**) and **decir** (**dir-**). As with the future, the endings of the conditional are the same for regular and irregular verbs.

A couple of final comments about the usage of the conditional are in order. First, the conditional is used in Spanish, as in English, to form a more polite request:

Me **gustaría** una copa de vino.   *I would like a glass of wine.*

There is one usage of the conditional in Spanish that corresponds to one use of *would* in English that is not truly conditional in that it does not express a consequence of a hypothetical. The conditional in both languages can be used to express *probability in the past* as well as to express the future when in a past context. In the first case, the conditional answers to the common English verb *to wonder*, but when used in the past. In the latter case, the conditional may be substituted by the imperfect of the formula **ir** + **a** + infinitive. In English questions, the conditional *would* is usually expressed as *could*. Consider the following examples of the use of the conditional:

¿Dónde **estaría** Juan?   *I wonder where John was.*
                                      Where could John have been?

¿Qué **estaría** haciendo Teresa en   *I wonder what Theresa was doing just*
    ese momento?   *then.*
                                      What could Theresa have been up to
                                          just then?

¿Qué hora **sería** cuando Juan te llamó? *I wonder what time it was when John*
                                          called you.
                                      What time could it have been when John
                                          called you?

Juan me dijo que **vendría** a eso de *John told me he would come around five*
    las cinco.   *o'clock.*

This last usage of the conditional to indicate an action that is future yet in the past can also be rendered using the familiar **ir** + **a** + infinitive formula, using the imperfect indicative:

Juan me dijo que **iba** a venir a eso de *John told me he was coming around five*
    las cinco.   *o'clock.*

Since the conditional is often presented before the imperfect subjunctive, the latter tense and mood will be supplied in many of the statements in the following exercises. In addition, only the simple, or one-word, form of the conditional will be required in the answers.

Fill in the blanks with the proper form of the verbs in parentheses, using the conditional. In the case of reflexives, don't forget to include the proper form of the pronoun in the blank.

1. (hacer) ¿Qué _____ tú en mi lugar?

2. (ver) Si fueras al norte de Alaska, ¿qué _____ ?

3. (tener) Para ganar dinero con este plan, nosotros _____ que invertir demasiado.

4. (querer) Juana _____ invitarlo a la fiesta, pero es que Carlos _____ sacarla a bailar.

5. (decir) Si ellos fueran honestos, _____ la verdad.

6. (declarar) El Congreso _____ la guerra contra cualquier país que nos atacara.

7. (ponerse) Si hiciera calor, yo no _____ el suéter.

8. (poder) Si tú tuvieras veintiún años, _____ acompañarme al bar.

9. (saber) Si el comité entendiera algo sobre las Artes, _____ que su plan es tonto.

10. (ir) Yo no _____ a esa ciudad nunca, aun si me pagaran el vuelo y el hotel.

11. (gustar) Me _____ comer en ese restaurante, pero no tengo suficiente tiempo.

12. (haber) ¿Crees tú que _____ paz en el mundo si nadie estuviera muriendo de hambre?

13. (sentarse) Ella _____ en el parque si no fuera de noche.

14. (salir) En caso de incendio, claro, nosotros _____ inmediatamente.

15. (pensar) ¿En qué _____ los Fundadores en 1776?

16. (recibir) Con una inversión tan grande, ellos _____ muchos dividendos.

17. (venir) Ellas saben que Juan está aquí, porque de lo contrario, _____ a nuestra fiesta.

18. (pagar) Sin empleo, ¿cómo crees que nosotros _____ las cuentas?

19. (valer) Creo que _____ la pena ir de excursión a las Pirámides de Egipto.

20. (esperar) Si ella fuera mi novia, yo la _____ con paciencia.

21. (buscar) ¿Qué _____ Juan Ponce de León? – Ah, ¡la Fuente de la Juventud!

22. (perder) Si ellos jugaran contra los Yankees, _____ sin duda.

23. (saber) A ver, ¿los vikingos _____ algo sobre la navegación en el hemisferio del sur?

24. (conocer) Si de veras hubiera vivido en Seattle, él _____ Pike's Market mejor.

25. (entender) Juan y Teresa _____ la lección si hubieran asistido a clase esta semana.

26. (encontrar) Si yo buscara en mi cuarto, _____ mi billetera.

27. (oír) En el planeta Marte, ¿cree que _____ nuestra estación de radio favorita?

28. (morirse) Con una dosis tan fuerte, hasta _____ un caballo.

29. (volver) Con tan poco que perder y tanto que ganar, ellos _____ a invertir su dinero.

30. (empezar) Si ellos realmente tuvieran un plan, _____ a ponerlo por obra.

EJERCICIO
7·2

Dehydrated sentences. *Use the following elements, making whatever additions and changes necessary to create grammatically correct sentences using the conditional.*

1. yo/no ir/a ese lugar/porque/ser peligroso.

   _____

2. tú y Carlos/salir/en caso de emergencia.

   _____

3. ¿ellos/saber/la verdad/en ese momento?

   _____

4. con tanta lluvia/ellos/ponerse/impermeable.

   _____

5. en tu lugar, yo/ir/fiesta.

   _____

6. Juan/venir/pero/no poder.

   _____

7. ella/querer/vaso de agua.

   _____

8. si fueran honestos/ellos/decir/verdad.

   _____

9. en una granja/yo/tener que/ordeñar/vacas.

   _____

10. Juan/tener/cinco años/en 1969.

    _____

11. yo/poder/hacerlo/pero no hay tiempo.

    _____

12. haber/guerra/en caso de un ataque.

    _____

13. hace buen tiempo, pero si no/ellas/salir.

    _____

14. ellos/poder/ayudarme/mañana.

    _____

15. a ella/gustar/tomar/refresco.

    _____

16. tú/venir/fiesta/si tuvieras tiempo.

    _____

17. ellos/comprar/ropa/con/tarjeta de crédito.

    _____

18. él/ponerse/corbata/si fuera una ocasión formal.

_____

19. ¿qué/hacer/tú/en su lugar?

_____

20. yo/no decirle/mentiras/papá.

_____

21. ¿qué/pensar/Ud./en mi lugar?

_____

22. no valer/pena/subir/montaña.

_____

23. ella/hacer/vestido/pero no tiene tiempo.

_____

24. me/gustar/pasar más tiempo/hija.

_____

25. ¿viajar/tú/Antártida?

_____

26. chicos/hacer viaje/pero/no permitirlo/padres.

_____

27. ella/ponerse/zapatos/si hiciera frío.

_____

28. yo/no poder/hacerlo/ni por todo el oro del mundo.

_____

29. Uds./salir/pero hay que trabajar.

_____

30. nosotros/ir/Roma/si el vuelo no costara tanto.

_____

Preterit system 1

Preterit indicative

8

The third microsystem gives us the fourth principal part and consists solely of the **yo** form or first-person singular of the *preterit indicative* of any given verb, regular or irregular. After the present system, the preterit microsystem is arguably the most important for the derivation of verb forms because through it both the *preterit indicative* and the *imperfect subjunctive* are derived.

Most students are puzzled by the irregularities they encounter in the preterit simply because these irregularities do not follow the patterns they struggled to learn for the present tense. By learning the **yo** form in the preterit indicative, you will be alert to the pattern that particular verb follows in that tense and mood and, as you'll see in the next chapter, with a little trick, you'll be able to instantly give all the forms of that verb in the imperfect subjunctive.

The first thing to know about the formation of the preterit is that there are four main types or patterns: *regular* verbs, *single-vowel stem irregulars*, *new-stem irregulars*, and *uniquely irregulars*. In the case of regular verbs, there is one set of endings for the **-ar** verbs and one set in common for **-er** and **-ir** verbs. We saw this phenomenon before when we examined the imperfect indicative (the other past tense), but the endings in the preterit are quite different. Let us examine the endings for verbs that are regular in the preterit indicative:

hablar		comer		vivir	
hablé	hablamos	comí	comimos	viví	vivimos
hablaste	hablasteis	comiste	comisteis	viviste	vivisteis
habló	hablaron	comió	comieron	vivió	vivieron

The first features that should attract your attention as you study the patterns of the preterit are that, once again, the -**mos** and -**n** are markers for the first- and third-person plural endings. Gone, however, is -**s** as a marker for the **tú** form. But, thankfully, the -**ste** pattern takes its place in all three families of verbs. Furthermore, the endings of the regular forms of the first- and third-persons singular are stressed on the final vowel, unlike the present tense. This is an important feature, since **hablo** means *I* *speak* but **habló** means *he, she,* or *you* (formal) *spoke*. Likewise, the difference between **hablé** (*I spoke*) and **hable** (first- and third-person singular of the present subjunctive and also the **Ud.** command) are distinguishable in speaking and writing only by the stressed or unstressed vowel. Additionally, the **nosotros** forms of the -**ar** and -**ir** verbs are indistinguishable from their present indicative, meaning that context, such as other words in a sentence, will reveal if they are present or preterit. This is not true of the -**er** verbs, since their preterit endings are identical to the preterit endings of -**ir** verbs and thus cannot be mistaken for any other tense.

The second group, the *single-vowel stem irregulars*, consists of two subgroups. The first group includes verbs that in the present tense exhibit an **e** → **i** stem change in the shoe pattern of the present system but now only show this change in their third-person forms. The second group, **morir** and **dormir**, have a stem change of **o** → **ue** in a shoe pattern in the present but now only show **o** → **u** in their third-person forms. The following examples summarize these two slight irregularities:

pedir		dormir	
pedí	pedimos	dormí	dormimos
pediste	pedisteis	dormiste	dormisteis
p**i**dió	p**i**dieron	d**u**rmió	d**u**rmieron

The third group, the *new-stem irregulars*, consists of a considerable number of high-frequency verbs. Thus it is important to memorize their respective **yo** forms, or fourth principal part. It is also extremely important to note that these new-stem irregulars, whether or not they are -**ar**, -**er**, or -**ir**, have *one* set of endings in common. The model verb used in TurboVerb, **tener**, is one such verb and was chosen for that reason. Observe its six principal parts, taking particular notice of its fourth one, **tuve**. (As a matter of fact, the inspiration for TurboVerb, and ultimately this book, came about entirely one day when I was explaining to a student that there is nothing about the infinitive or present tense forms of **tener** that can be used to predict this new stem of **tuv-**. This gave rise to the adoption and adaptation of the principal parts method for learning Spanish verbs.) The full conjugation of **tener** in the preterit reveals the endings shared by *all* verbs with *new stems* in the preterit:

tuv**e**	tuv**imos**
tuv**iste**	tuv**isteis**
tuv**o**	tuv**ieron**

Besides sharing a common set of endings, note that in no person or number of the conjugation of the new-stem irregulars is there a final stressed syllable, unlike what was observed in the regular verbs. Following is a useful enumeration of the most high-frequency verbs of this type, listed by their infinitives and their first-persons singular in the preterit. These new-stem verbs may be subdivided further, according to the patterns revealed in the previous groupings. Note that the first group has an **-i-** in the new stem, the second group is characterized by **-uv-**, the third by **-u-**, and, for verbs with infinitives ending in **-ucir**, **-uj-**. The fourth group is often called the "j-stem" group. The j-stem verbs are slightly different from the others in only one way: their third-person plural form drops the -i- from its ending (e.g., **dijeron**).

hacer	hice
querer	quise
venir	vine
andar	anduve
estar	estuve
tener	tuve
caber	cupe
haber	hube
poder	pude
poner	puse
saber	supe
conducir	conduje
decir	dije
traducir	traduje
traer	traje

Finally, the *uniquely irregular verbs* in the preterit indicative include **ser** and **ir** (whose forms are identical in this tense and mood) and **dar**. **Ser** and **ir** are best memorized as vocabulary items, but once their forms are known, their principal parts will remind you of their pattern. Even though they are identical in the preterit, the context is almost always different enough that you can be fairly certain you'll always know which verb is being used:

fui	fuimos
fuiste	fuisteis
fue	fueron

The verb **dar** is conjugated as if it were a regular -er or -ir verb. One way to remember its form, in addition to simply learning its fourth principal part, is to recall that its preterit forms rhyme with the preterit forms of **ver**, which is regular:

dar		**ver**	
di	dimos	vi	vimos
diste	disteis	viste	visteis
dio	dieron	vio	vieron

Next, verbs whose infinitives end in **-car**, **-gar**, and **-zar** undergo a spelling change to preserve the pronunciation of the consonants at the end of their stem, but only in the first-person singular of their preterit indicative forms. We encountered this same group in the present subjunctive. The change there is identical except that the final syllable of their first-person preterit form is stressed. The difference between the present subjunctive forms and the preterit is that all persons and numbers of their present subjunctive forms have this change since consonant changes in the **yo** form are preserved throughout. Once again, the pronunciation of these preterit forms sounds regular. If Spanish had no written form, they would be regular. Note that **-zar** verbs no longer have any change in the vowel of their stem; this change is limited to the present in all cases. It is helpful to regard these verbs as sounding regular, but their spelling has to be changed to reflect this regularity:

buscar		pagar		empezar	
bus**qué**	buscamos	pa**gué**	pagamos	empe**cé**	empezamos
buscaste	buscasteis	pagaste	pagasteis	empezaste	empezasteis
buscó	buscaron	pagó	pagaron	empezó	empezaron

Since the preterit focuses on an action in the past, when the verbs **querer**, **poder**, **saber**, and **conocer** are in the preterit, their meanings change. The following examples summarize these differences:

Quise abrir la ventana, pero no pude.   *I tried to open the window, but failed to do so.*

Juana no **quiso** salir con Tomás.   *Jane refused to go out with Tomás.*

Cuando **supe** eso, perdí el habla.   *When I found out about that, I was speechless.*

Juan la **conoció** en la fiesta anoche.   *John met her at the party last night.*

EJERCICIO
8·1

Fill in the blanks with the proper form of the verbs in parentheses, using the preterit. In the case of reflexives, don't forget to include the proper form of the pronoun in the blank.

1. (poder) Juan corrió a la estación, pero no _____ llegar a tiempo.

2. (ir) Ellos _____ al parque por dos horas.

3. (decir) Yo no le _____ nada ayer.

4. (querer) ¿_____ tú hacer la tarea?

5. (huir) El ladrón _____ cuando oyó el gatillo.

6. (estar) ¿Dónde _____ tú ayer a las tres?

7. (ponerse) Yo _____ el sombrero y salí en seguida.

8. (ser) Julio César _____ dictador del Imperio Romano.

9. (conducir) Ellos _____ por cinco horas sin parar.

10. (saber) Nosotros sólo lo _____ a la última hora.

11. (perder) Se dice que «Puchacay» es el lugar donde el diablo _____ su sombrero.

12. (aparecer) El fantasma _____ enfrente de la chimenea.

13. (sentirse) Al oír esto, Elena _____ muy triste.

14. (dormirse) Los niños estaban tan cansados que _____ en seguida.

15. (pagar) Yo se lo _____ ayer y en efectivo.

16. (pedir) Juan _____ la mano de Teresa anoche.

17. (pensar) Cuando me lo contó, yo _____ que estaba loco.

18. (servir) Las meseras me _____ mucho café esta mañana.

19. (caerse) Los alpinistas _____ 10 metros antes de recuperarse.

20. (buscar) Yo te _____ por una hora.

21. (traer) Juan no _____ traje, así que no nadó.

22. (decir) Nosotros les _____ todos los detalles en la reunión ayer.

23. (estar) Yo _____ en la biblioteca esperándote a las cuatro.

24. (poder) ¿_____ tú arreglar la motocicleta?

25. (repetir) Su mamá le _____ dos veces lo que ella quería.

26. (hacer) Yo no _____ la tarea porque no me sentía bien.

27. (oír) De repente, ellos _____ un grito.

28. (ver) Yo te _____ en la calle.

29. (dar) Yo te lo _____ ayer.

30. (saber) ¿Cuándo lo _____ tú?

Dehydrated sentences. *Use the following elements, making whatever additions and changes necessary to create grammatically correct sentences using the preterit.*

1. yo/no tener tiempo/la semana pasada.

_____

2. ese señor/decirnos/la verdad.

_____

3. yo/no verte/dos días.

_____

4. ellos/traer/libros/biblioteca.

_____

5. ellas/querer/llamarme/vez.

_____

6. él/andar/de un lado al otro/ciudad.

_____

7. ¿quién/darme/este regalo?

_____

8. ¡yo/no hacerlo!

_____

9. niña/ponerse/la falda antes de salir anoche.

_____

10. ellos/poder/escalar/montaña después de cuatro días.

   _____

11. maestra/definir/palabra/clase ayer.

   _____

12. yo/decírselo/en las barbas.

   _____

13. Juana/escribirme/carta/amor.

   _____

14. ella/saberlo/por teléfono.

   _____

15. él/empezar/reír.

   _____

16. conejos/huir/de los perros.

   _____

17. ¿para qué/servirle/a Juan estudiar tanto?

   _____

18. yo/conocerte/hace dos años.

   _____

19. ¿quién/traducir/estas cartas?

   _____

20. ella/pedirme/beso.

   _____

21. obreros/construir/puente.

   _____

22. yo/pagarle/lo que le debía.

   _____

23. ella/dormir/diez horas.

_____

24. profesor/salir/clase/tres/tarde.

_____

25. nosotros/trabajar/una semana.

_____

26. yo/venir/Seattle/2001.

_____

27. Uds./repetirle/instrucciones.

_____

28. Ud./ponerse/triste/escuchar las noticias.

_____

29. tú/estar/esperar/a las dos.

_____

30. yo/no buscarte/hasta las tres.

_____

Preterit system 2

Imperfect subjunctive

Once you know the preterit forms, you're in for a treat. The most delightful feature of the principal parts method lies in the elegance of its utility. Being able to derive verb forms without memorizing each person and number, referenced to the infinitive, is liberating and makes the study of Spanish exciting and vibrant. The secret to the derivation of the *imperfect subjunctive* from the preterit lies in the fact that no matter how irregular a verb might be in the preterit indicative with respect to its infinitive or present tense forms (its other principal parts), the imperfect subjunctive is formed in a smooth, perfectly predictable pattern from the third-person plural of the preterit indicative.

If you refer to TurboVerb, you'll see how this applies to **tener**, our model verb. Let's try deriving the imperfect subjunctive of a uniquely irregular preterit form, **ser/ir**. The preterit form of both, you'll remember, is:

fui	fuimos
fuiste	fuisteis
fue	**fuer**on

Remember this rule: Use the third-person plural form of any preterit verb (in this case **fueron**), remove the **-on** and substitute it with **-a**, and begin conjugating, using this form as the **yo** form of the imperfect subjunctive. This gives you the imperfect subjunctive of **ser/ir**:

fuera	fuéramos
fueras	fuerais
fuera	fueran

Try another verb or as many as you wish. Consult any reference work that reveals all the conjugations of hundreds of verbs. You'll discover that you now have a very powerful tool indeed. Let's try another verb, **conducir**, and work from its third-person plural, **condujeron**:

condujera	condujéramos
condujeras	condujerais
condujera	condujeran

The one patterned difference we see in the imperfect subjunctive is that, as we've seen so often, the first- and third-persons singular are identical.

There is another set of endings for the imperfect subjunctive, usually reserved for formal writing but sometimes also encountered in speech. It also is derived from the third-person plural of the preterit indicative, but instead of substituting the final -**on** with -**a**, the ending -**se** (not to be confused with the pronoun **se**) plus personal endings is used. Just to put the value of the systematic use of the principal parts method to the test, let's try an -**ar** and an -**ir** verb:

hablar		decir	
hablase	hablásemos	dijese	dijésemos
hablases	hablaseis	dijeses	dijeseis
hablase	hablasen	dijese	dijesen

As promised in a previous chapter, there is a *future subjunctive* and a *future perfect subjunctive* (for the latter, consult Chapter 11). While it is unlikely that you will need to use these forms, if you intend to study classical Spanish literature, or if you should encounter proverbs or read a legal document, it is important to recognize them. To form the future subjunctive, use the -**a** form of the imperfect subjunctive but substitute the -**a** with an -**e**. Again proceed conjugating from this new **yo** form, adding the personal endings, as seen with **tener**:

tuviere	tuviéremos
tuvieres	tuviereis
tuviere	tuvieren

One example of the use of the future subjunctive is found in the following proverb:

Cuando **fueres** a Roma, haz como los romanos.	*When you go to Rome, do as the Romans.*

This proverb is also found in a modern form, which shows that the present subjunctive has assumed the role of the future subjunctive, at least in everyday speech:

Cuando **vayas** a Roma, haz como los romanos.	*When you go to Rome, do as the Romans.*

The future subjunctive is also common in some boilerplate phrases in contracts, such as the following:

...quien en su poder lo **tuviere**...	*. . . in whomsoever's possession it shall be . . .*

Let's recall one special usage of the imperfect subjunctive. Just as the conditional is often used to create polite requests, so too is the imperfect subjunctive. When used with the helping verbs **deber**, **querer**, and **poder** the imperfect subjunctive creates statements or questions that are even more polite. There is no adequate translation into English to reflect this most polite form without sounding childish or "over the top" in your courtesies, but this form is quite important socially. Examine the following examples of increasingly polite statements or requests:

Flat questions or statements, not rude, but unadorned

¿**Puedes** acompañarme a la playa?	*Can you go to the beach with me?*
Debes estudiar más.	*You should study more.*
¿**Quieres** un café?	*Do you want a coffee?*

More polite

¿**Podrías** acompañarme a la playa?	*Could/Would you be able to go to the beach with me?*
Deberías estudiar más.	*You ought to study more, honestly.*
¿**Querrías** un café?	*Would you care for a coffee?*

Most polite, essentially untranslatable

¿**Pudieras** acompañarme a la playa?
Debieras estudiar más.
¿**Quisieras** un café?

EJERCICIO
9·1

Fill in the blanks with the proper form of the verbs in parentheses. Start with verbs in the appropriate past indicative tense and then use the imperfect subjunctive. In the case of reflexives, don't forget to include the proper form of the pronoun in the blank.

1. (decir/decir) Su mamá le _____ que _____ la verdad siempre.

2. (buscar/hacer) Nosotros _____ un artesano que _____ figuras de madera.

3. (decir/tener) Yo te _____ que _____ cuidado.

4. (esperar/querer) Ud. _____ que ella te _____ .

5. (insistir/ser) Ellas _____ en que él _____ despedido.

6. (dudar/andar) Tú _____ que él _____ tanto tiempo en la nieve sin zapatos.

7. (recomendar/ponerse) Tú me _____ que _____ un abrigo.

8. (ser/ir) ¡_____ magnífico que tú _____ a Madrid para estudiar!

9. (alegrarse/poder) Yo _____ de que Juana y Teresa _____ venir a mi fiesta.

10. (creer/saber) Ella no _____ que su novio _____ que le había engañado con Pedro.

11. (esperar/perder) Yo _____ que tú no _____ la carrera de los 400 metros.

12. (gustar/parecerse) Nos _____ que ella _____ a una actriz famosa.

13. (preferir/venir) Ella _____ que ellos no _____ a su casa con el perro.

14. (querer/sentarse) Tú _____ que los niños _____ en una mesa aparte.

15. (aconsejar/dormir) El médico me _____ que _____ ocho horas todas las noches.

16. (querer/pedir) Ella _____ que su novio _____ su mano en el restaurante.

17. (dudar/pensar) En ese momento, yo _____ que ella _____ en nuestro bien.

18. (decir/servir) Ella me _____ que no les _____ el chocolate a los niños.

19. (tener/caerse) Juan _____ miedo de que su perro _____ al río.

20. (preferir/volar) Mi papá siempre _____ que nosotros _____ a Europa.

21. (insistir/jugar) La maestra _____ en que los niños no _____ en clase.

22. (ser/tocar) ¡_____ fantástico que tú _____ el piano anoche!

23. (buscar/saber) Yo _____ un mecánico que _____ arreglar mi coche.

24. (dudar/llover) Ellos _____ que _____ .

25. (buscar/entender) La compañía _____ una secretaria que _____ chino y árabe.

26. (mandar/construirse) El presidente _____ que _____ una base militar allí.

27. (dar/oír) Me _____ pena que tú _____ esto de tu propio amigo.

28. (entristecerse/morirse) Ellos _____ de que su actor favorito

_____ en ese momento.

29. (recomendar/hervir) El cocinero nos _____ que _____ la sopa por 20 minutos.

30. (decir/traducir) Te _____ ayer que _____ esta carta urgente.

EJERCICIO
9·2

Dehydrated sentences. *Use the following elements, making whatever additions and changes necessary to create grammatically correct sentences using the imperfect subjunctive. Be careful to put main verbs in the appropriate indicative past tense and watch out for hypothetical statements in which the conditional is used to express the consequence of an* if *clause.*

1. si ella/casarse/Juan/no tener hijos/cinco años.

   _____

2. tú/insistir/ayer/yo/hacer/torta.

   _____

3. si nosotros/ir/Chicago/tener frío.

   _____

4. ella/dudar/tú y yo/ser/novios.

   _____

5. ellas/no alegrarse/yo/recibir/ascenso.

_____

6. yo/bañarme/antes de que/tú/venir/mi casa.

_____

7. mi hermana/esperar/yo/llamarla/anoche.

_____

8. si ella/volver a pedir/yo/aceptar/oferta.

_____

9. Juan/explicarlo/para que/ellos/entenderlo.

_____

10. nosotros/decidir salir/con tal de que/Teresa/venir también.

_____

11. ella/ponerse/suéter/en caso de que/hacer frío.

_____

12. si tú/venir/divertirnos mucho más.

_____

13. ellos/practicar/para que/tú/escuchar/buen concierto.

_____

14. ella/recomendarme/visitar/Museo del Vaticano.

_____

15. su mamá/insistir/hijo/vestirse solo.

_____

16. tú buscar/fotógrafo/poder filmar/partido de baloncesto.

_____

17. nosotros querer/tú/poner/mesa.

_____

18. ella/insistir/amigos/no hacer ruidos/fiesta.

_____

19. mi amigo/preferir/tú y yo/no conocer/hermana.

_____

20. yo/esperar/tú/no esperarme.

_____

21. si tú/ir/Europa/ver/museos famosos.

_____

22. astronautas/temer/aparecer/extraterrestres.

_____

23. ellos/dudar/haber vida/otros planetas.

_____

24. ella/buscar/amiga/traer/pastel.

_____

25. Jaime/necesitar/computadora/poder tocar música.

_____

26. yo no querer/ella/ponerse/vestido.

_____

27. no agradarme/ella/traicionar/colegas.

_____

28. ayer/no haber nadie aquí/saber pilotar avión.

_____

29. profesor/querer/alumnos/tomar/clase de poesía.

_____

30. si yo/tener suerte/ganar/lotería.

_____

Participial system 1

Gerunds

In English, the *gerund* form is the verb with the *-ing* ending. Its use in English and Spanish is similar, but not identical. The chief function of this fifth principal part is to form the progressive aspect in all tenses. Most textbooks tend to limit their coverage of the progressive aspect to the present and the past and show how the verb **estar** is used to form this aspect, e.g., **estoy comiendo** (*I am eating*). In this chapter, we're going to expand on both the forms and uses of the gerund as an adverb, as an adjective, and of its progressive aspect.

First of all, the gerund form is sometimes called the *present participle*, but that is a bit of a misnomer. The present participle is technically a different form (e.g., **sapiente** vs. **sabiendo**). The former is the present participle of the verb **saber** and is used as the adjective: *wise* (literally, *being wise*), whereas **sabiendo** is the gerund—the only form that can be used to form the progressive aspects of verbs in various tenses.

The gerund is easy to form and is mostly regular, although two types of irregularities in the present microsystem do "float over" to this principal part. In fact, we have encountered these verbs before. This is the second principal part wherein some verbs' irregular stems have anything to do with an irregularity in another microsystem (the other was in the third-person singular and plural of the preterit for *single-vowel stem irregulars*). Fortunately, these are minor annoyances because there are only a handful of high-frequency verbs whose gerund form is irregular. There is more good news in that no consonant stem irregularities found in the present system resurface in the gerund.

There are two forms of gerund endings, one for **-ar** verbs and one in common for **-er** and **-ir** verbs. Once again, you can be glad to know that the endings are unaffected by any irregularities found in the verb stems. To form the gerund, remove the infinitive endings; for **-ar** verbs, add **-ando** to the end of the stem and for **-er** and **-ir** verbs, add the ending **-iendo**. For verbs whose stem ends in vowel, the **-i-** of the gerund ending is changed to a **-y-** for spelling purposes. Observe the following examples, beginning with the three model regular verbs:

hablar	→	hablando
comer	→	comiendo
vivir	→	viviendo
leer	→	leyendo
creer	→	creyendo
ir	→	yendo

To form the gerund of irregular verbs, refer to the derivation rules in the fourth column of TurboVerb (participial microsystem). As noted earlier, you'll notice that the verbs whose gerund forms are irregular consist of those whose present indicative forms have a stem change involving a single vowel (**e → i**), plus **herir** and **hervir** (**e → ie** in their present tense forms, but **e → i** for their gerunds), along with **dormir** and **morir**. These latter two verbs have a stem change resulting in a diphthong in the present tense, but their gerund forms have only a single vowel change (**o → u**). Observe how the gerund of these verbs is formed:

decir	→	diciendo	dormir	→	durmiendo
hervir	→	hirviendo	morir	→	muriendo
pedir	→	pidiendo			
repetir	→	repitiendo			
servir	→	sirviendo			

Besides being used with **estar** and a few other helping verbs to form the periphrastic progressive aspect in all tenses and moods, the gerund has other functions. When not used to form a progressive, its function is essentially adjectival or adverbial, the adverbial usage being more frequent:

Adjectival
El niño regresó a casa **llorando**.   *The little boy came home crying.*

Adverbial
El niño vino **corriendo** a su mamá.   *The little boy came running to his mother.*

The gerund forms of two verbs, **arder** (**ardiendo**) and **hervir** (**hirviendo**), have become adjectives in their own right, in certain situations.

Cuidado con el horno **ardiendo**.   *Be careful with the burning oven.*
Hay una olla de aceite **hirviendo**   *There's a pot of boiling oil on the stove.*
en la estufa.

The progressive, an *aspect*, not a tense, is used to emphasize an action as being in progress. The *tense* of the progressive depends wholly on the tense of the helping verb, most frequently, the verb **estar**. Since the imperfect indicative is the form used to show action in progress in the past, it is sometimes redundant to use the imperfect of **estar** + gerund. However, if you are intentional about drawing attention to the ongoing nature of an action in the past, it is precisely what you need to use. Compare the following, noting that they both translate the same way into English:

Juan **corría** por el parque ayer cuando alguien le robó la mochila.	*Juan was running through the park yesterday when someone robbed him of his backpack.*	Juan **estaba corriendo** por el parque ayer cuando alguien le robó la mochila.

The difference between the two sentences in Spanish is that the second one is more vivid and would probably be told in an excited tone of voice. The function of the gerund construction is to draw attention to the ongoing action. The first sentence is a bit more matter of fact. The difference, therefore, between English and Spanish is that while the vividness of the English sentence could only be evoked with tone, Spanish has the option of using a progressive verb phrase on top of an already progressive, one-word form.

From the psychological point of view of Spanish speakers, English speakers tend to overuse the progressives when speaking Spanish. This could be because the progressive is so easy to form and technically only requires that you know the various tenses of **estar**, or it could be due to the fact that English uses the progressive more often than Spanish. Whatever the reason, English speakers are advised to reserve the progressives for emphatic or vivid statements and use them judiciously. Overusing the progressives can impart a sense of urgency or even hyperactivity. Consider these two options for a question on the telephone. The English translations are meant to impart the feeling implicit in the verb forms of the question:

¿Qué **estás haciendo** ahora?	*What are you doing right this very moment?*
¿Qué **haces**?	*What's up?*

Obviously, both forms have a time and a place, but if you're just interested in small talk or in hanging out, you should use the second option. Let's consider how similar differences in a conversation about the past can also have connotations that are easily missed by English speakers:

¿Qué **estabas haciendo** ayer por la tarde?	*What, exactly, were you up to yesterday afternoon?*
¿Qué **hacías** ayer por la tarde?	*What were you doing yesterday afternoon?*

Depending on other contextual clues, tone, and so forth, the first example could be taken as an accusatory question. The second is more down to earth. Even in print, without tone, the difference is due to the unnecessary verbal complexity of the first. It's a bit like when you were a kid and heard your mother or father call you by your full name—you *knew* you were in trouble!

As mentioned earlier, the progressive aspect can appear in any tense and mood. Observe the following examples:

Mañana **estaremos trabajando** toda la tarde.	*Tomorrow, we'll be working all afternoon.*
Mañana **vamos a estar trabajando** toda la tarde.	*Tomorrow, we're going to be working all afternoon.*

Dudo que Juan **haya estado trabajando** hoy.	*I doubt John has been working today.*
No dudo que Juan **está trabajando** ahora.	*I don't doubt John is working now.*

In addition to being used to form progressives in any time frame, other helping verbs commonly used instead of **estar** include **ir**, **andar**, **venir**, **seguir**, **continuar**, and **quedar**. The most common, in widespread use in Mexico, is **quedar**. Its progressive aspect usually denotes the ongoing outcome of a completed action. In this context, it is synonymous with **permanecer**:

Los atletas **quedaron practicando** el resto del día.	*The athletes stayed practicing for the rest of the day.*

When used with verbs of perception, thought, or depiction, the gerund can be used to refer to the direct object. When used in this way, it is equivalent to a relative clause. Such verbs include **sentir**, **ver**, **oír**, **observar**, **distinguir**, **hallar**, **pintar**, **grabar**, and **representar**. Compare the following sentences:

¿No oyes a los pájaros **cantando** en las ramas?	*Don't you hear the birds singing in the trees?*
¿No oyes a los pájaros **que cantan** en las ramas?	*Don't you hear the birds that sing in the trees?*

In the last example, the relative clause **que cantan** has replaced the gerund used in the first example. In passing, note that most English speakers would probably use the progressive in the relative clause and thus say *that are singing*. If the Spanish example had been **que están cantando**, it would have been to focus deliberately on the ongoing nature of the singing.

Finally, let me offer you three reminders about gerunds. First, they have no gender and thus are invariable in form. Secondly, when you need to use a verbal noun, use the infinitive, *not* the gerund, as English does. Last of all, object pronouns either precede their helping verbs or can be attached to the end of the gerund with an accent on the stressed syllable. The following two examples show the use of the gerund as an adverb of manner (**cantando**), and the infinitive as a verbal noun (**jugar**):

La niña camina a casa **cantando**.	*The little girl walks home singing.*
Jugar al baloncesto es su deporte favorito.	*Playing basketball is his favorite sport.*

Most Spanish speakers would probably say the last example a bit differently:

Su deporte favorito es **jugar al baloncesto**.	*His favorite sport is playing basketball.*

Remember also that when object pronouns are used with gerunds, they may precede the auxiliary verb or be placed after, and attached to, the gerund. The difference is stylistic.

| Alfredo **me lo estaba diciendo**. | *Alfred was telling me that.* |
| Alfredo **estaba diciéndomelo**. | |

Remembering that infinitives can be used as subjects may also help you master the use of the verb **gustar**. Thus, when in English we say that a person *likes to do* something, in Spanish the subject of the verb **gustar** is an infinitive:

A Juana **le gusta ir de compras**.	*Jane likes going shopping.*
	Jane likes shopping.
	Jane likes to shop.

Note that there is only one exercise in this chapter because it incorporates the problem of the few irregular gerund forms, the use of the progressive in all tenses and moods, and employs the most common helping verbs used to form the progressives.

EJERCICIO
10·1

Fill in the blanks with the verbs in parentheses to form the progressive aspect. Note that the progressive is not limited to the present tense, nor is it formed only with **estar***, so pay attention to temporal clues. In the case of reflexives, don't forget to include the proper form of the pronoun in the blank.*

1. (ir, hablar) Ayer mi amigo _____ consigo mismo mientras caminaba.

2. (seguir, ser) Aun después de estudiar el cálculo, _____ difícil por un rato.

3. (estar, decir) ¿No entiendes lo que yo te _____ ?

4. (seguir, querer) Aun después de que ella lo abandonó, él la _____ .

5. (estar, vestirse) ¡No entres! Yo _____ .

6. (estar, ponerse) Su papá entró en el cuarto cuando sus hijos _____ las botas.

7. (ir, cantar) Vi que mi novia _____ mientras se bañaba.

8. (estar, volar) El único vuelo que sale mañana _____ a Tegucigalpa.

9. (estar, repetirle) Hijo, sabes cuánto me molesta tener que _____ todo.

10. (quedarse, trabajar) El jefe se fue, y nosotros _____ .

11. (ir, perder) ¡Uf! Este partido es una pérdida de tiempo: ese equipo _____ toda la tarde.

12. (continuar, jugar) Cuando la maestra los dejó solos, los chicos _____ .

13. (estar, sentirse) Ay, amiga, no quiero que tú _____ mal por culpa de él.

14. (estar, hablar) El pintor no quería que nosotros _____ cerca de su lugar de trabajo.

15. (estar, ver) Ella es tan bella que no puedo creer lo que yo _____ .

16. (seguir, pedir) Me molestó que ellas nos _____ el mismo favor.

17. (quedarse, dormir) La Bella Durmiente del Bosque _____ por 100 años.

18. (estar, servir) Veo que en este restaurante los meseros ya _____ la cena.

19. (seguir, caerse) No pudo abrir el paracaídas, así que _____ hasta dar con la tierra.

20. (irse, volar) Cuando oí el disparo, yo _____ para no estar en la calle.

21. (estar, tener) Ya veo que ese niño _____ problemas en la escuela.

22. (estar, enfermarse) Lentamente, todos _____ debido a un derrame de un gas tóxico.

23. (quedarse, leer) Su papá fue un ignorante: no quería que su hijo _____ todo el tiempo.

24. (seguir, creer) A pesar de las pruebas, hay gente que _____ en supersticiones.

25. (estar, morir) Cuando su abuelo _____ , él vivía en otro país.

26. (estar, construir) Muy pronto nosotros _____ una regadera en la Logia.

27. (seguir, oír) Después del incendio, Juan _____ las sirenas por una hora.

28. (estar, dormir) ¿Por qué me despertaste? ¿No viste que yo _____ ?

29. (continuar, hervir) Se nos olvidó la olla y _____ hasta evaporarse toda el agua.

30. (estar, traducir) A lo mejor, esta noche, ella _____ otros documentos importantes.

Participial system 2

The seven perfect tenses

The *past participle*, also called the *passive participle*, is the second of the two forms found in the participial microsystem and the last of the six forms you need in order to master the principal parts method presented in TurboVerb. The main use of this principle part is to form the seven Spanish tenses that require the use of the helping verb **haber**. They are known as the perfect tenses because the actions they refer to are completed with respect to some other temporal frame of reference. Sometimes you'll see them called the compound tenses as well. Observe the following comparisons of *simple* tenses and *perfect* tenses:

Ella **come** ahora.	*She is eating now.*
Ella ya **ha comido.**	*She has eaten already.*
Yo **jugué** al tenis ayer.	*I played tennis yesterday.*
Yo **había jugado** al tenis cuando llegaste ayer.	*I had played tennis when you arrived yesterday.*

For all intents and purposes, the temporal logic needed to use the perfect tenses of English and Spanish is identical. There are three hurdles to overcome in order to use the tenses correctly in Spanish. First, you need to learn the twelve irregular past participles. Next, you must learn the forms of **haber** in its seven *simple* tenses, which are used with participles to form the seven *perfect* tenses. The last hurdle deals with the possibility that you don't use the perfect tenses correctly in English. Of the three, the last problem is the stickiest because improper use of the perfect tenses is rampant in American English and old habits die hard.

To solve the first problem, memorize the six principle parts of the twelve verbs that have irregular past participles, found also in TurboVerb. Please note that I did not say to memorize the twelve irregular participles independently of the other principle parts of these verbs. The beauty of the system depends specifically on keeping all forms in their proper relationships with each other. Thus, your homework is to learn these twelve verbs using the principle parts format; note that the italics merely show the form that this chapter is concerned with:

abro, abres; abrir; abrí; abriendo, *abierto*
cubro, cubres; cubrir; cubrí; cubriendo, *cubierto*

digo, dices; decir; dije; diciendo, *dicho*
escribo, escribes; escribir; escribí; escribiendo, *escrito*
hago, haces; hacer; hice; haciendo, *hecho*
imprimo, imprimes; imprimir; imprimí; imprimiendo, *impreso*
muero, mueres; morir; morí; muriendo, *muerto*
pongo, pones; poner; puse; poniendo, *puesto*
resuelvo, resuelves; resolver; resolví; resolviendo, *resuelto*
rompo, rompes; romper; rompí; rompiendo, *roto*
veo, ves; ver; vi; viendo, *visto*
vuelvo, vuelves; volver; volví; volviendo, *vuelto*

All compounds of these verbs are also irregular in the same manner as the verbs upon which they are built. Thus, **absolver** forms its past participle the same as **resolver** forms its (both being built from **solver**, a verb that is now all but obsolete).

Regular past participles are formed by changing -**ar** to -**ado** and both -**er** and -**ir** to -**ido**. Thus, our traditional models for regular verbs give us:

hablar	hablado
comer	comido
vivir	vivido

Again, the seven perfect tenses are formed by using the seven simple tenses of the helping verb **haber**, whose forms also are found on TurboVerb. The logic is very simple. Each of the seven simple tenses of any given verb has its corresponding perfect tense, formed by the same simple tense of **haber** for that tense, plus the invariable past participle.

In order to illustrate this succinctly, let's look at a synoptic conjugation, that is, one that shows all the forms of only one person and number. Let's use the **tú** form of the verb **decir**, whose past participle is irregular. Notice how the only thing that changes is the form of the helping verb **haber**; in these examples you'll see **haber** change only because of the changes in tense. Keep in mind that there are five other forms for **haber** in each tense and mood.

dices	*you say*	has dicho	*you have said*
digas	*[that] you say*	hayas dicho	*[that] you have said*
decías	*you were saying*	habías dicho	*you had said*
dijiste	*you said*	hubiste dicho	*you had said*
dijeras	*[that] you would say*	hubieras dicho	*[that] you had said*
dirás	*you will say*	habrás dicho	*you will have said*
dirías	*you would say*	habrías dicho	*you would have said*

If you take a close look at these examples, you'll see that the indicative and subjunctive forms of the seven simple tenses are displayed on the left side and their corresponding perfect tenses and moods are on the right. Except in certain dialects or in all dialects when explicitly referring to a moment in time, the perfect tense formed with the *preterit* of **haber** (**hube**, **hubiste**, etc.) is not common in speech; therefore, it has essentially the same meaning as the one formed with the imperfect indicative (**había**, **habías**, etc).

The other detail to note is that the subjunctive form **dijeras**, called the *imperfect subjunctive*, is used when either the imperfect or preterit indicatives need to "turn into" subjunctives. One way to think of this is to regard the imperfect subjunctive as "one past subjunctive that corresponds to the two indicative aspects of the past." The present perfect subjunctive has a one-to-one relationship with its indicative form. To prove this, compare the following sentences and you'll see that, in terms of tense, the present perfect indicative and the present perfect subjunctive translate only one way into English. This is because modern English only rarely has dedicated forms for the subjunctive:

Veo que Juan **ha comido**.	*I see that John has eaten.*
Dudo que Juan **haya comido**.	*I doubt that John has eaten.*

It may come as a shock to some, but these examples show that the subjunctive has no meaning—it is, truthfully, merely a form that is needed in certain constructions. The tense of the subjunctive, when it is needed, depends on the tense of the main verb. Compare the previous examples with these:

Vi que Juan **comía**.	*I saw that John was eating.*
Dudaba que Juan **comiera**.	*I had my doubts that John would eat.*
Dudé que Juan ya **hubiera comido**.	*I doubted that John had eaten already.*

Lastly, let's examine the use of the *future perfect* and the *conditional perfect*. There is a sort of inside joke among grammarians that says that "the future perfect is a tense that one will not have needed in one's whole life." If you can remember that little joke, or this next one, you will have mastered the idea of the future perfect. It is formed by the simple future forms of **haber** plus the past participle of any given verb. The need to use the future perfect depends on when some future action or event will occur relative to a later future point of reference, such as the hour:

Para las cinco, **habré terminado** este capítulo.	*By five o'clock, I will have finished this chapter.*

As you learned in Chapter 6, the simple future is used to ask questions and make statements, such as English does with the verb *to wonder*, as well as to make probability statements in general. The future perfect can also do this, but the probability of the event or action in question is more distant in the future and will often be specifically related to some other future moment. Consider this example, which could be worded in a number of ways, but serves to show the use of the future perfect to make probability statements:

Para las diez, ¿**habremos recibido** la información sobre la cuenta?

I wonder if by ten o'clock we will have received the information about the account.

It may seem overly simplistic to say this, but the conditional perfect is used in Spanish whenever *would have* + a past participle is used in English. Any further difficulties an English speaker might encounter in using it correctly in Spanish are likely due to improper use of this construction in English. One of the most common and therefore important uses of the conditional perfect is found in what are variously labeled as *counterfactual* statements, *contrary-to-fact* statements, or *hypothetical* statements. All refer to the same type of construction, and all involve an *if* clause. The conditional perfect must always be used to express the consequence of an *if* clause, or hypothetical statement shifted into the past, in which case the *if* clause must be expressed using the *pluperfect subjunctive*. Compare the following sentences:

Hypothesis in the present

Si Juan **fuera** a México, **aprendería** el español pronto.

If John went to Mexico, he soon would learn Spanish.
If John were to go to Mexico, he soon would learn Spanish.

Hypothesis in the past

Si Juan **hubiera** ido a México, **habría aprendido** el español pronto.

If John had gone to Mexico, he soon would have learned Spanish.

You also learned in Chapter 7 that the conditional can be used to express futurity when in a past time frame. Here's a fresh example that, contrasted with the use of the conditional perfect, shows how the use of the latter tends to be limited to hypotheticals, whether fully stated or not:

Decidí que **iría** al concierto después de cenar.

I decided that I would go to the concert after dinner.

Había decidido ir al concierto, y **habría ido** si **hubieras podido** acompañarme.

I had decided to go to the concert, and would have gone, if you could have gone with me.

Habríamos cenado en el centro, pero...

We would have had dinner downtown, but . . .

In the same chapter, you also learned about the use of the conditional to express some uses of the verb *to wonder* as well as to make probability statements in the past. The conditional perfect also performs this function, but the probability is in a more remote past. In English, *could* or *would* can be used to express this probability:

¿**Habría dejado** un mensaje de voz antes de que yo **llegara** a la oficina?

Could he possibly have left a voice message before I got to the office?

All the perfect tenses, except the *preterit anterior* (**hube**, **hubiste**, etc. + past participle) will be required at least once in the fill-in-the-blank exercises, so there is only one set of exercises for this chapter. ¡**Buena suerte!**

EJERCICIO
11·1

Fill in the blanks with the proper form of the verbs in parentheses, using the appropriate perfect tense, that is, the correct form of the verb **haber** + past participle. *The helping verb* **haber** *has not been listed in parentheses, since it is being called for in each sentence. Watch for the contextual clues to determine the time frame. In the case of reflexives, don't forget to include the proper form of the pronoun in the blank.*

1. (decir) Es dudoso que ellos _____ la verdad hasta ahora.

2. (imprimir) La editorial _____ el libro si el editor no hubiera creído que era mentira.

3. (cubrir) Yo _____ la olla para que no se enfríe la sopa.

4. (vivir) Si esa compañía te hubiera contratado, _____ en Puerto Rico por dos años ya.

5. (volver) Me pregunto si tu hermana _____ ya del Perú.

6. (hacer) Habrías ganado mucho más dinero si _____ algo con la tecnología.

7. (abrir) Habríamos podido vender este modelo si _____ la tienda antes de las ocho.

8. (ir) Busco una novia que _____ alguna vez a México.

9. (resolver) Fui a la oficina con prisa, pero supe que ellos _____ el problema.

10. (poner) Se me arruinó el reloj porque lo _____ donde luego se cayó en el lavabo.

11. (ver) Me alegro de que ellos _____ la película recientemente.

12. (escribir) Antes de que termine la guerra, muchos _____ sus memorias.

13. (romperse) El tanque _____ si lo hubiéramos levantado sin ti.

14. (morirse) Esperamos ir a ver a nuestro bisabuelo con tal de que no _____ .

15. (hacer) ¿Qué _____ tú con la vida si no te hubieras casado conmigo?

16. (imprimir) Ella habría tenido un problema con el jefe si _____ la carta.

17. (volver) Cuando me levanté esta mañana, vi que tú _____ de las vacaciones.

18. (saber) Cuando ella esté de nuevo en casa luego, _____ sobre el accidente.

19. (poner) Yo sé que María _____ la ropa en la secadora porque puedo oír el motor.

20. (morirse) Cuando todos llegaron al hospital, su bisabuelo ya _____ .

21. (decir) Para las cinco mañana, tú ya _____ todo lo que se necesita decir.

22. (abrir) Tuve que esperar esta mañana, porque el gerente todavía no _____ la tienda.

23. (poner) Avísenos cuando ya _____ la mesa porque tenemos hambre.

24. (cubrir) Se pegó la sopa en la olla; la _____ si hubiera sabido que pudiera pasar esto.

25. (romper) ¡Oye, pero _____ mi bicicleta, amigo!

26. (escribir) Si yo no _____ ese mensaje, habríamos tenido que seguir su plan ridículo.

27. (resolver) Espero que cuando yo llegue esta tarde, ella _____ la dificultad con Carlos.

28. (decir) Si ella _____ algo para revelar que el plan era ridículo, yo la habría respetado.

29. (ver) ¿_____ tú un eclipse del sol alguna vez?

30. (hacer) Cuando te gradúes, ya _____ mucho para prepararte para tu carrera.

Participipial system 3

Passive participles

Thus far, we have seen the use of this last of the six principle parts, the *past participle*, to form the seven perfect tenses. Now we shall explore why this form is also called the *passive participle*.

The name *participle* itself reveals the dual use of this form. It is said to *participate* in a language sometimes as a verb, as in the previous chapter, and sometimes as an adjective (a simple adjective or predicate adjective or to form the passive voice). The two participles in this fourth and last microsystem each have distinctive functions in terms of what is known as *voice*. Whereas the gerund is an active construction, the past participle, when functioning as an adjective, is passive. The following two examples will help make this clear, particularly if you recall that when the participle **abierto** is used with **haber** to form any of the perfect tenses, it translates into English as *opened*, not as the adjective *open*:

Estoy abriendo las ventanas.	*I am opening the windows.*
Las ventanas **están abiertas**.	*The windows are open.*

When used as a verb, this participle has no gender markers or indication of number because the person and number are revealed by the helping verb **haber**. In this chapter, however, the participle is acting in its various roles as an *adjective* and so it will have gender and number, as in the second example. To appreciate that the passive participle performs fully as an adjective, consider these following sentences. Observe how the passive participles are used as predicate adjectives, agreeing in gender and number with the nouns they modify. This is easy to see by comparing the nouns in the main clauses, that is, before **estar**, the *be* verb:

La tienda **está abierta**.	*The shop is open.*
Las puertas **están abiertas**.	*The doors are open.*
El salón **está cerrado**.	*The salon is closed.*
Los teléfonos **están rotos**.	*The telephones are broken.*

Spanish is an adjective-poor language in the sense that it has relatively fewer "pure" adjectives such as **bonito** and **feo**. It makes up for this lexical shortfall efficiently by enlisting the passive participles of verbs into this role. That's why, in Spanish, we say **enojado** for *angry*, for instance. It literally means *angered*.

It is customary when presenting passive participles to remark on their use with **estar** and **ser**. One of the most pervasive and pernicious errors about using **ser** or **estar** generally, and in particular with adjectives, is to assert that "**ser** is for permanent things and **estar** is for temporary things." This is simply wrong. One example should dispel this mistake:

Julio César está muerto.	*Julius Caesar is dead.*

There is a key to explaining this and to help you make the right decisions when faced with **ser**, **estar**, and an adjective. The verb **estar** is used with adjectives *to indicate a change of state or condition*. No matter what your religion, being dead is pretty permanent, so the usage here is best explained as being due to showing a change of state or condition from living to dead.

One way to remember this little rule is to notice that the English noun *state* and the Spanish verb **estar** are derived from the same Latin verb: **stare**.

Likewise, since we are born single, it is the condition you are in until you get married, at which time there is a *change* in your civil status. Hence, we say in Spanish:

Juan y Enrique **son** solteros.	*Joe and Henry are bachelors.*
Tomás **está casado** pero su hermana **está divociada**.	*Thomas is married but his sister is divorced.*

Some adjectives change meaning, depending on whether they are used with **ser** or **estar**. Examples of these are **cansado** and, in a more subtle way, **casado**:

Juan **está cansado**.	*John is tired.*
Juan **es cansado**.	*John is boring.*

Next, consider this brief and somewhat saucy dialogue:

—¿**Está** casado ese hombre?	*—Is that guy married?*
—Sí.	*—Yes.*
—Ah, bueno, pero... ¿*es* casado?	*—Oh, well, but is he . . . married?*

Due to the nature of the two *be* verbs themselves, there are other issues about the use of **ser** and **estar** with adjectives that lie outside the scope of their use with passive participles. In general, the most useful notion is to keep in mind that a change of state or condition is the cue that **estar** is the right choice to make *when drawing attention to that change*. For instance, the general rule is that **ser** is to be used when expressing a person's age, but if you haven't seen someone for a long time and note that he or she has aged, you would use **estar**. Compare these two sentences:

| Mi abuelo **es** viejo. | *My grandfather is old.* |
| ¡Ay, abuelo, pero qué viejo **estás**! | *Goodness, grandpa, but you've aged!* |

Finally, just as **estar** is the verb used with gerunds to form the progressive aspects in the various tenses and moods, **ser** is the verb used with passive participles to form the passive voice in the various tenses and moods. In order to understand this clearly, compare the following three sentences, all telling the story of a simple event in the past, but in the *active voice*, *passive voice*, and, finally, the *impersonal*, or *se construction*:

Active voice

| Los niños **rompieron** las ventanas. | *The boys broke the windows.* |

Passive voice

| Las ventanas **fueron rotas** por los niños. | *The windows were broken by the boys.* |

Se construction

| **Se rompieron** las ventanas. | *The windows got broken.* |

The active voice gives a more true-to-life statement in that the boys are the subjects, the ones who did the breaking, and the windows received that action. The passive voice turns the real actors into passive agents, putting the focus on the windows. Finally, the **se** construction shifts the focus from the real doers of the active voice and even omits the boys as passive agents. The focus is on the action and its result. Of the three types of sentences, the active voice and the **se** construction are more common in Spanish than the true passive.

Notwithstanding the relatively less frequent usage of the true passive voice in Spanish, it is still important. This last example shows that the passive participle is functioning as a predicate adjective with **ser** as the copulative verb, just as our first examples of the use of passive participles as predicate adjectives at the beginning of this chapter used **estar** as the copulative verb. In both cases, the passive participles have to agree with the noun they modify in person and number, hence **ventanas** and **rotas** in the example of the passive voice.

EJERCICIO

12·1

Change the following sentences from active to passive voice. Be careful not to change the tense, just the voice.

1. El gerente abrió la tienda a las nueve.

   _____

2. El carpintero hace muebles.

   _____

3. Vimos un barco de vela.

_____

4. Yo escribiré unas cartas.

_____

5. Mi hermana hizo unas tortas.

_____

6. Tú has puesto el paquete en la mesa.

_____

7. Nosotros resolvemos problemas todos los días.

_____

8. Su madre cubrió las macetas de flores.

_____

9. Ella dirá la verdad.

_____

10. Dudo que ellos hayan puesto la computadora en la oficina.

_____

11. Ese chico romperá los juguetes.

_____

12. Ojalá hayas impreso los artículos que necesito.

_____

Translate the following passive voice sentences from English to Spanish.

1. The packages have been received by John.

_____

2. The car will be repaired by his brother.

_____

3. The pillows were made by my grandmother.

_____

4. The letters were written by us.

_____

5. The bicycle was broken by him.

_____

6. The gifts will be opened by the children.

_____

7. The movie was seen by everyone.

_____

8. The truth has been told by her.

_____

9. The shop was closed by Mr. Gómez.

_____

10. The house was sold by Ms. Reyes.

_____

11. The food was prepared by our friends.

_____

12. The bathroom was cleaned by Mr. Ramírez.

_____

APPENDIX A

TurboVerb™

The "better mousetrap" for learning Spanish verbs

I designed TurboVerb for students in their second or third semester of Spanish. Typically, such students are being exposed to or have been exposed to the whole verb system. Frequently, the exposure has been quick, and students confuse the various patterns of regular and irregular verbs not only within each tense but between the tenses, giving rise to erroneous hybrids such as **tengara**, **sabara**, and so on.

Teachers and students often wish there were some sort of teaching tool that would work like a fine-tooth comb and sort out the various types of irregularity tense by tense. Often, teachers recommend different printed reference works dealing with verbs in order to accomplish this morphological repair. But what often happens is that students feel overwhelmed by the number of forms each verb can take. While reference works are excellent for learning usage rules and for looking up the form of a specific verb, provided the student knows which to look up, from a pedagogical point of view in teaching the forms of the tenses, they are weak. When a student has seen all the tenses and has improperly digested them, the physical presentation of Spanish verbs in these works usually confuses him or her more, because it is precisely the overall patterns the student does not see that is causing the mixing and combining of verb stems and endings that they do recall but combine haphazardly. One could say that these lengthy reference works give students a basket of fish but don't teach them how to fish. These morphological confusions can be avoided by employing the principle parts method from day one in the first year of study, or solved by using it in a fourth quarter or third semester of Spanish.

How to use TurboVerb

TurboVerb is based on the ancient method of principle parts, used for millennia to teach Spanish's mother tongue, Latin. I have adapted this system to the peculiarities of Spanish to create TurboVerb. With the handful of derivation rules found in each of its four microsystem columns, only six forms of every verb need be memorized in order to accurately find any form of any verb. It's like having an entire reference work in your head for the price of six forms! In fact, only five verbs need to be learned separately: **dar**, **estar**, **haber**, **ir**, **saber**, and **ser**.

Each of the four columns correspond to the four microsystems of the Spanish verb macrosystem: the present, the infinitive, the preterit, and the participial systems. Within each microsystem, there are rules for deriving the tenses and moods that are morphologically related. Each tense and mood is identified by name.

There are fourteen tenses in Spanish in addition to the infinitive, the imperatives, and two participles. With TurboVerb, students learn the first- and second-person singular of the present indicative, the infinitive, the first-person singular of the preterit, and the two participles (more accurately, the passive participle and the gerund)—a total of six forms. The derivation rules within each of these four systems enable learners to derive those tenses and moods, which are based on the idiosyncrasies of that microsystem. This information is presented in column format, permitting the derivation of all persons and numbers of the remaining twelve tenses as well as the imperatives.

From the infinitive, the imperfect indicative, the future, and the conditional are derived. From the first person of the preterit, not only are all persons and numbers of this tense derived, but also the imperfect subjunctive. Finally, the participial system contains two invariable forms. By knowing the forms of **estar** and using them with the gerund, all the progressive forms are found. Likewise, by knowing all the simple tenses of the helping verb **haber**, all seven compound tenses may be formed.

All irregular forms within any given system are revealed within each column in TurboVerb, thus helping students avoid mixing which irregularities of any given verb apply to the tense they are seeking.

Note: The method for deriving verb forms modeled by the following TurboVerb chart works for all verbs except **dar**, **estar**, **haber**, **ir**, **saber**, and **ser**, which must be learned separately.

TurboVerb™

Present System

(pres. ind.) tengo, tienes

(pres. subj.) tenga, tengas

Irregular Vowel Patterns*

o → ue

poder	puedo	podemos
	puedes	podeís
	puede	pueden

e → ie

tener	tengo, tienes...
entender	entiendo, entiendes...

u → ue

jugar	juego, juegas...

e → i

servir	sirvo, sirves...
pedir	pido, pides...
decir	digo, dices...

Irregular Consonant Patterns**

tener	tengo, tienes...
decir	digo, dices...
conocer	conozco, conoces...

*Single vowel to diphthong irregularity: *shoe* pattern in the present system (present indicative and present subjunctive). Single vowel to single vowel (**e → i**), *shoe* pattern in the present indicative *only*, in all persons in the present subjunctive.

In the present subjunctive: -car**, -**gar**, -**guar**, -**zar** → -**que**, -**gue**, -**güe**, -**ce**; -**ger**, -**gir**, -**guir**, -**quir** → -**ja**, -**ja**, -**ga**, -**ca**; vowel + -**cer**, -**cir** → -**za**; consonant + -**cer**, -**cir** → -**zca**; -**asir** → -**asga**

Consonant or single-vowel irregularities: in all persons/numbers of imperatives and present subjunctive. If both exist in the **yo** form, both appear. Consonant irregularities override diphthong ones (compare **tener**, **decir**, and **servir**).

Infinitive System

ten*er*

(imp. ind.) tenía…

Only 3 verbs are irregular in the imperfect:

ser	era…
ir	iba…
ver	veía…

(fut.) tendr…

(cond.) tendría…

Only twelve verbs have irregular stems in the future and conditional:

decir	dir-
hacer	har-
poner	pondr-
salir	saldr-
tener	tendr-
valer	valdr-
venir	vendr-
caber	cabr-
haber	habr-
querer	querr-
saber	sabr-
poder	podr-

Preterit System

(pret.) tuve...
(imp. subj.) tuviera...

Many verbs have irregular stems in the preterit. **Ir** and **ser** are identical and, along with **haber,** their forms generally must be memorized separately.

Verbs whose present indicative are **e → i** or **o → u** show this irregularity in the third-person forms only (sing. and pl.).

By definition, all forms of the imperfect subjunctive are regular; all persons and numbers being derived directly from the third-person plural of the preterit, thus:

tuve	tuvimos
tuviste	tuvisteis
tuvo	tuvier**on**

tuvier**a**	tuviéramos
tuvieras	tuvierais
tuviera	tuverian

In other words, simply replace **-on** with **-a,** then continue the conjugation using the personal endings.

Note that verbs with irregular stems in the preterit, such as **tener,** have their own set of endings. Although **dar** is an **-ar** verb, it follows the pattern of regular **-er/-ir** verbs.

Participial System

tenido*
teniendo**

*Used as adjectives generally or, with **haber,** as passive participles. Regulars formed thus: **ar → ado; -er/-ir → ido**. Irregulars include the following and all their derivatives:

abrir	abierto
absolver	absuelto
cubrir	cubierto
decir	dicho
escribir	escrito
hacer	hecho
imprimir	impreso
morir	muerto
poner	puesto
resolver	resuelto
romper	roto
ver	visto
volver	vuelto

Used with **estar, seguir, quedar, ir, continuar to form progressive aspect (-*ing*).

Regulars: **-ar → ando; -er/ir → -iendo**.

Irregulars: verbs whose present indicative are irregular: **e → i** or **o → u**: d**i**ciendo, m**u**riendo, p**i**diendo, rep**i**tiendo, s**i**rviendo; and **i → y** when between vowels: le**y**endo, cre**y**endo.

Regular Tense Endings and Important Verbs

Tense Endings			**haber**	
pres.	-o	-amos	he	hemos
	-as	-áis	has	habéis
	-a	-an	ha	han
	-o	-emos		
	-es	-éis		
	-e	-en		
	-o	-imos		
	-es	-ís		
	-e	-en		
imp.	-aba	-ábamos		
	-abas	-abais		
	-aba	-aban		
	-ía	-íamos	había	habíamos
	-ías	-íais	habías	habíais
	-ía	-ían	había	habían
pret.*	-é	-amos		
	-aste	-asteis		
	-ó	-aron		
	-í	-imos	hube	hubimos
	-iste	-isteis	hubiste	hubisteis
	-ió	-ieron	hubo	hubieron
fut.	-é	-emos	habré	habremos
	-ás	-éis	habrás	habréis
	-á	-án	habrá	habrán
cond.	-ía	-íamos	habría	habríamos
	-ías	-íais	habrías	habríais
	-ía	-ían	habría	habrían
pres. subj.	-ar → e + personal endings		haya	hayamos
	-er/-ir → a + personal endings		hayas	hayáis
			haya	hayan
imp. subj.	Derived *regularly* from third-person plural preterit. (See previous page under "Preterit System.")		hubiera	hubiéramos
			hubieras	hubierais
			hubiera	hubieran

---

*For verbs with irregular stems in the preterit, use the endings of **haber** (see also **tener** on the previous page under "Preterit System").

Present System	Infinitive System	Preterit System	Participial System
hablo, hablas...	hablar	hablé	hablado, hablando
como, comes...	comer	comí	comido, comiendo
vivo, vives...	vivir	viví	vivido, viviendo
hago, haces...	hacer	hice	hecho, haciendo
escojo, escoges...	escoger	escogí	escogido, esogiendo
pongo, pones...	poner	puse	puesto, poniendo
traigo, traes...	traer	traje	traído, trayendo
dirijo, diriges...	dirigir	dirigí	dirigido, dirigiendo
quiero, quieres...	querer	quise	querido, queriendo
veo, ves...	ver	vi	visto, viendo
muero, mueres...	morir	morí	muerto, muriendo
sirvo, sirves...	servir	serví	servido, sirviendo
río, ríes...	reír	reí	reído, riendo
rompo, rompes...	romper	rompí	roto, rompiendo
sigo, sigues...	seguir	seguí	seguido, siguiendo
digo, dices...	decir	dije	dicho, diciendo
huelo, hueles...	oler	olí	olido, oliendo
conozco, conoces...	conocer	conocí	conocido, conociendo
entrego, entregas...	entregar	entregué	entregado, entregando
comienzo, comienzas...	comenzar	comencé	comenzado, comenzando
identifico, identificas...	identificar	identifiqué	indentificado, identificando
doy, das...	dar	di	dado, dando
averiguo, averiguas...	averiguar	averigüé	averiguado, averiguando
dilinco, dilinques...	delinquir	delinquí	delinquido, delinquiendo
conduzco, conduces...	conducer	conduje	conducido, conduciendo
vengo, vienes...	venir	vine	venido, viniendo

Imperatives

Pers./No.	ir	ver	ser	tener	dar
+ vosotros	id	ved	sed	tened	dad
+ tú	ve	ve	sé	ten	da
+ Ud.	vaya	vea	sea	tenga	dé
+ Uds.	vayan	vean	sean	tengan	den
– Uds.	no vayan	no vean	no sean	no tengan	no den
– Ud.	no vaya	no vea	no sea	no tenga	no dé
– tú	no vayas	no veas	no seas	no tengas	no des
– vosotros	no vayáis	no veáis	no seáis	no tengáis	no deis

	entregar	comenzar	verificar	conocer	saber
+ vosotros	entregad	comenzad	verificad	conoced	sabed
+ tú	entrega	comienza	verifica	conoce	sé
+ Ud.	entregue	comience	verifique	conozca	sepa
+ Uds.	entreguen	comiencen	verifiquen	conozcan	sepan
– Uds.	no entreguen	no comiencen	no verifiquen	no conozcan	no sepan
– Ud.	no entregue	no comience	no verifique	no conozca	no sepa
– tú	no entregues	no comiences	no verifiques	no conozcas	no sepas
– vosotros	no entreguéis	no comencéis	no verifiquéis	no conozcáis	no sepáis

APPENDIX B

Survival verbs

The following is a list of useful verbs for everyday life, arranged alphabetically according to the Spanish infinitives, the third principle part in this model. This arrangement helps learners distinguish between many verbs that look alike and are often confused, such as those beginning with **ll**-.

The thematic tendency of this list is somewhat toward a focus on business, school, and office situations. It is intended to be a starter list for using the principal parts method, so users should be aware that the definitions given are only "first level," such as may be found in the first word shown in a bilingual dictionary. For instance, **manejar**, whose meaning is listed as *manage*, can also mean *to drive* or, in a shop, it can mean *to carry*, as in "We don't carry that item." Thus, as a simple list, it cannot offer clues about usage, distinguish between verb pairs (such as **ser** and **estar**), or show whether a verb can be reflexive. One exception has been made in the case of **sentarse** to contrast it with **sentir** (which also can be reflexive).

Note that some verbs do not work perfectly with the principle parts system, but they have been included on this list due to their great importance: **dar**, **estar**, **haber**, **ir**, **saber**, and **ser**. Please note how this model of the principal parts method works, using the English verb *to go* as a key. The word *to* has been omitted in the following list, alphabetized according to the Spanish infinitives, in which the English meanings of the verbs are shown to the left.

go	**I go, you go; to go; went; going, gone**
open	abro, abres; abrir; abrí; abriendo, abierto
rent	alquilo, alquiles; alquilar; alquilé; alquilando, alquilado
love	amo, amas; amar; amé; amando, amado
approve	apruebo, apruebas; aprobar; aprobé; aprobando, aprobado
increase	aumento, aumentas; aumentar; aumenté; aumentando, aumentado
verify	averiguo, averiguas; averiguar; averigüé; averiguando, averiguado
dance	bailo, bailas; bailar; bailé; bailando, bailado
erase	borro, borras; borrar; borré; borrando, borrado
fit	quepo, cabes; caber; cupe; cabiendo, cabido
fall	caigo, caes; caer; caí; cayendo, caído
cook	cocino, cocinas; cocinar; cociné; cocinando, cocinado
begin	comienzo, comienzas; comenzar; comencé; comenzando, comenzado
buy	compro, compras; comprar; compré; comprando, comprado
conclude	concluyo, concluyes; concluir; concluí; concluyendo, concluido
drive	conduzco, conduces; conducir; conduje; conduciendo, conducido
know	conozco, conoces; conocer; conocí; conociendo, conocido
count	cuento, cuentas; contar; conté; contando, contado
hire	contrato, contratas; contratar; contraté; contratando, contratado
convince	convenzo, convences; convencer; convencí; convenciendo, convencido
agree to	convengo, convienes; convenir; convine; conviniendo, convenido
create	creo, creas; crear; creé; creando, creado
believe	creo, crees; creer; creí; creyendo, creído
cover	cubro, cubres; cubrir; cubrí; cubriendo, cubierto
give	doy, das; dar; di; dando, dado
ought, owe	debo, debes; deber; debí; debiendo, debido
say, tell	digo, dices; decir; dije; diciendo, dicho
leave, let	dejo, dejas; dejar; dejé; dejando, dejado
desire	deseo, deseas; desear; deseé; deseando, deseado
fire	despido, despides; despedir; despedí; despidiendo, despedido
direct	dirijo, diriges; dirigir; dirigí; dirigiendo, dirigido
diminish	disminuyo, disminuyes; disminuir; disminuí; disminuyendo, disminuido
sleep	duermo, duermes; dormir; dormí; durmiendo, dormido
throw	echo, echas; echar; eché; echando, echado
wrap	embalo, embalas; embalar; embalé; embalando, embalado
worsen	empeoro, empeoras; empeorar; empeorando, empeorado
employ	empleo, empleas; emplear; empleé; empleando, empleado
emphasize	enfatizo, enfatizas; enfatizar; enfaticé; enfatizando, enfatizado

understand	entiendo, entiendes; entender; entendí; entendiendo, entendido
enter	entro, entras; entrar; entré; entrando, entrado
hand over	entrego, entregas; entregar; entregué; entregando, entregado
send	envío, envías; enviar; envié; enviando, enviado
chose	escojo, escoges; escoger; escogí; escogiendo, escogido
write	escribo, escribes; escribir; escribí; escribiendo, escrito
listen	escucho, escuchas; escuchar; escuché; escuchando, escuchado
be	estoy, estás; estar; estuve; estando, estado
evaluate	evalúo; evalúas; evaluar; evalué; evaluando, evaluado
exclude	excluyo, excluyes; excluir; excluí; excluyendo, excluido
export	exporto, exportas; exportar; exporté; exportando, exportado
manufacture	fabrico, fabricas; fabricar; fabriqué; fabricando, fabricado
please	gusto, gustas; gustar; gusté; gustando, gustado
have (aux.)	he, has; haber; hube; habiendo, habido
make	hago, haces; hacer; hice; haciendo, hecho
mortgage	hipoteco, hipotecas; hipotecar; hipotequé; hipotecando, hipotecado
import	importo, importas; importar; importé; importando, importado
print	imprimo, imprimes; imprimir; imprimí; imprimiendo, impreso
include	incluyo, incluyes; incluir; incluí; incluyendo, incluido
inform	informo, informas; informar; informé; informando, informado
involve	involucro, involucras; involucrar; involucré; involucrando, involucrado
go	voy, vas; ir; fui; yendo, ido
wash	lavo, lavas; lavar; lavé; lavando, lavado
read	leo, lees; leer; leí; leyendo, leído
lift	levanto, levantas; levantar; levanté; levantando, levantado
call	llamo, llamas; llamar; llamé; llamando, llamado
arrive	llego, llegas; llegar; llegué; llegando, llegado
fill	lleno, llenas; llenar; llené; llenando, llenado
carry, wear	llevo, llevas; llevar; llevé; llevando, llevado
order, send	mando, mandas; mandar; mandé; mandando, mandado
manage	manejo, manejas; manejar; manejé; manejando, manejado
maintain	mantengo, mantienes; mantener; mantuve; manteniendo, mantenido
kill	mato, matas; matar; maté; matando, matado
measure	mido, mides; medir; medí; midiendo, medido
improve	mejoro, mejoras; mejorar; mejoré; mejorando, mejorado
lie	miento, mientes; mentir; mentí; mintiendo, mentido
put in(to)	meto, metes; meter; metí; metiendo, metido
look at	miro, miras; mirar; miré; mirando, mirado
die	muero, mueres; morir; morí; muriendo, muerto

need	necesito, necesitas; necesitar; necesité; necesitando, necesitado
hate	odio, odias; odiar; odié; odiando, odiado
hear	oigo, oyes; oír; oí; oyendo, oído
pay	pago, pagas; pagar; pagué; pagando, pagado
seem	parezco, pareces; parecer; parecí; pareciendo, parecido
request	pido, pides; pedir; pedí; pidiendo, pedido
hit, stick	pego, pegas; pegar; pegué; pegando, pegado
think, plan	pienso, piensas; pensar; pensé; pensando, pensado
forgive	perdono, perdonas; perdonar; perdoné; perdonando, perdonado
permit	permito, permites; permitir; permití; permitiendo, permitido
weigh	peso, pesas; pesar; pesé; pesando, pesado
be able, can	puedo, puedes; poder; pude; pudiendo, podido
put	pongo, pones; poner; puse; poniendo, puesto
delay	postergo, postergas; postergar; postergué; postergando, postergado
predict	predigo, predices; predecir; predije; prediciendo, predicho
question	pregunto, preguntas; preguntar; pregunté; preguntando, preguntado
prepare	preparo, preparas; preparar; preparé; preparando, preparado
foresee	preveo, prevés; prever; preví; previendo, previsto
produce	produzco, produces; producir; produje; produciendo, producido
want	quiero, quieres; querer; quise; queriendo, querido
remove	quito, quitas; quitar; quité; quitando, quitado
edit, redact	redacto, redactas; redactar; redacté; redactando, redactado
reduce	reduzco, reduces; reducir; reduje; reduciendo, reducido
relate, tell	relato, relatas; relatar; relaté; relatando, relatado
yield	rindo, rindes; rendir; rendí; rindiendo, rendido
repeat	repito, repites; repetir; repetí; repitiendo, repetido
revise, check	reviso, revisas; revisar; revisé; revisando, revisado
break	rompo, rompes; romper; rompí; rompiendo, roto
know	sé, sabes; saber; supe; sabiendo, sabido
take out	saco, sacas; sacar; saqué; sacando, sacado
exit, go out	salgo, sales; salir; salí; saliendo, salido
follow	sigo, sigues; seguir; seguí; siguiendo, seguido
be	soy, eres; ser; fui; siendo, sido
sit	me siento, te sientas; sentarse; me senté; sentándome, sentado
feel, regret	siento, sientes; sentir; sentí; sintiendo, sentido
serve	sirvo, sirves; servir; serví; sirviendo, servido
bribe	soborno, sobornas; sobornar; sobornando, sobornado
delete	tacho, tachas; tachar; taché; tachando, tachado

have	tengo, tienes; tener; tuve; teniendo, tenido
translate	traduzco, traduces; traducir; traduje; traduciendo, traducido
bring	traigo, traes; traer; traje; trayendo, traído
use	uso, usas; usar; usé; usando, usado
utilize	utilizo, utilizas; utilizar; utilicé; utilizando, utilizado
overcome	venzo, vences; vencer; vencí; venciendo, vencido
sell	vendo, vendes; vender; vendí; vendiendo, vendido
come	vengo, vienes; venir; vine; viniendo, venido
see	veo, ves; ver; vi; viendo, visto
verify	verifico, verificas; verificar; verifiqué; verificando, verificado
return	vuelvo, vuelves; volver; volví; volviendo, vuelto

Answer key

1 The Spanish verb system: An overview

1·1
1. <u>quiero</u>, quieres; <u>querer</u>; <u>quise</u>; queriendo, querido
2. veo, <u>ves</u>; <u>ver</u>; vi; viendo, <u>visto</u>
3. <u>digo</u>, dices; <u>decir</u>; dije; <u>diciendo</u>, dicho
4. abro, <u>abres</u>; abrir; abrí; abriendo, <u>abierto</u>
5. <u>pongo</u>, pones; <u>poner</u>; <u>puse</u>; poniendo, <u>puesto</u>
6. <u>hago</u>, <u>haces</u>; hacer; hice; haciendo, <u>hecho</u>
7. traigo, traes; <u>traer</u>; <u>traje</u>; trayendo, traído
8. <u>conozco</u>, conoces; conocer; <u>conocí</u>; conociendo, conocido
9. traduzco, <u>traduces</u>; <u>traducir</u>; <u>traduje</u>; traduciendo, traducido
10. sirvo, <u>sirves</u>; <u>servir</u>; serví; <u>sirviendo</u>, servido
11. hablo, <u>hablas</u>; <u>hablar</u>; <u>hablé</u>; hablando, hablado
12. busco, <u>buscas</u>; buscar; <u>busqué</u>; buscando, buscado
13. vivo, vives; <u>vivir</u>; viví; <u>viviendo</u>, vivido
14. <u>pido</u>, pides; <u>pedir</u>; pedí; <u>pidiendo</u>, pedido
15. <u>pierdo</u>, pierdes; <u>perder</u>; perdí; perdiendo, perdido
16. corro, <u>corres</u>; <u>correr</u>; corrí; corriendo, corrido
17. leo, <u>lees</u>; <u>leer</u>; leí; <u>leyendo</u>, leído
18. vuelvo, <u>vuelves</u>; volver; volví; volviendo, <u>vuelto</u>
19. escribo, escribes; <u>escribir</u>; escribí; escribiendo, <u>escrito</u>
20. <u>muerdo</u>, <u>muerdes</u>; morder; mordí; mordiendo, mordido
21. puedo, puedes; <u>poder</u>; <u>pude</u>; pudiendo, podido
22. <u>muero</u>, mueres; <u>morir</u>; morí; <u>muriendo</u>, <u>muerto</u>

23. como, <u>comes</u>; comer; comí; comiendo, <u>comido</u>

24. rompo, <u>rompes</u>; <u>romper</u>; rompí; rompiendo, <u>roto</u>

25. huelo, <u>hueles</u>; <u>oler</u>; olí; oliendo, olido

2   Present system 1: Present indicative

2·1   *The explanations provided for the first ten answers can be applied to the rest of the irregular verbs in this exercise, since they will fall into one of the patterns. If you have difficulty with this exercise, look up and write out the principal parts of each of the verbs and your confusion will disappear.*

1. Los niños <u>pueden</u> vestirse solos. *The verb **poder** is one of the most high-frequency verbs in Spanish and a prototype for all verbs that have a stem vowel irregularity in a shoe pattern of o → ue.*

2. Tú <u>eres</u> un estudiante muy talentoso. *The verb **ser** is one whose various forms in all tenses need to be memorized—its present tense forms don't work perfectly in the principal parts method.*

3. Yo siempre <u>digo</u> la verdad. *The verb **decir** is a high-frequency verb that exhibits both a consonant and a single-vowel stem change in the **yo** form, which makes knowing its principal parts very valuable.*

4. Ella <u>quiere</u> invitarlo a la fiesta. *The verb **querer** is also a high-frequency verb and a prototype of verbs that have a stem vowel irregularity in a shoe pattern of e → ie.*

5. Yo <u>huyo</u> de los engaños del mundo. *The irregularity of the verb **huir** is merely orthographical. In all words, if the letter i falls between vowels, it changes to a y.*

6. Él <u>está</u> en clase. *The irregularities of the verb **estar** in the present tense, both indicative and subjunctive, make it worth memorizing.*

7. Yo <u>me pongo</u> el impermeable si llueve.

8. Tú y yo <u>vamos</u> de compras mañana. *The present tense and most forms of **ir** show the value of using the principal parts method because it is impossible to guess its present tense based on its infinitive.*

9. Yo <u>conduzco</u> con cuidado en la ciudad. *The verb **conducir** is a good model for verbs with a consonant irregularity of c → zc in their **yo** form.*

10. ¿Qué <u>sé</u> yo de eso? *The **yo** form of **saber** is notoriously irregular and easily confused with the pronoun **se**, which is written without an accent.*

11. Los niños <u>pierden</u> la carrera.

12. Juana, es obvio que tú <u>te pareces</u> a tu mamá.

13. Ellos <u>se sienten</u> mal hoy por lo de ayer.

14. Yo <u>me siento</u> en esta silla, gracias.

15. Yo <u>aborrezco</u> los cuentos de aparecidos.

16. Ella nos <u>pide</u> un favor.

17. Ellos <u>piensan</u> que es ridículo comprar billetes de lotería.

18. Los meseros me <u>sirven</u> el pescado ahora.

19. La niña <u>se cae</u> en la acera de vez en cuando.

20. El avión <u>vuela</u> a San Francisco todos los días.

25. Parece que hoy hay menos que <u>entienden</u> la evolución que hace veinte años.

26. En mi ciudad, hay muchos hombres que <u>construyen</u> rascacielos.

27. Perdóname, pero yo no <u>oigo</u> bien.

28. ¿<u>Duermes</u> tú ocho horas todos los días?

29. El agua <u>hierve</u> cuando la temperatura alcanza los 100°C.

30. Yo <u>traduzco</u> documentos científicos todos los días.

2·2

1. Ella siempre le miente a su novio.

2. Yo les doy clases de inglés a los extranjeros.

3. Ella conduce como loca.

4. Yo salgo de clase temprano.

5. Ellas vienen de Los Ángeles.

6. Yo tengo que jugar con mi hija. *The verb **tener** is the main verb and so is the only verb conjugated. The **que** here is untranslatable and the verb **jugar**, as in English, remains in the infinitive.*

7. Yo puedo jugar al tenis. *The verb **poder** is the helping, or modal, verb and is the only one conjugated.*

8. Ella viene a Colombia.

9. Ud. puede manejar un carro. *The verb **poder** is the helping, or modal, verb and is the only one conjugated.*

10. Ellos saben tocar el piano. *The verb **saber**, when used as a helping verb, means "to know how to" and is therefore followed by an infinitive.*

11. Yo hago dibujos en el cuaderno.

12. Tú entiendes el discurso político.

13. Nosotros nos dormimos a las diez todas las noches.

14. Yo pongo el disco.

15. Tú quieres estudiar en Chile. *The verb **querer** is the helping, or modal, verb and is the only one conjugated.*

16. Mis hermanos piensan que tú tienes razón. *Here, the verb **pensar** introduces a subordinated clause, as should be evident from the second subject pronoun, **tú**. Thus, the word **que** must be inserted to connect them: "My brothers think <u>that</u> you are right."*

17. Ellos piensan viajar a Rapa Nui por el verano. *The verb **pensar** is the helping, or modal, verb and is the only one conjugated.*

18. Mi amigo sabe que yo digo la verdad.

19. Yo no sé hablar chino.

20. Tú quieres mudarte a Puerto Rico.

21. Yo sé que tú sabes la verdad. *The structure of this sentence follows the same pattern as Question 16.*

22. Juan se parece a su hermano.

23. Yo conozco a su hermana.

24. Ella enciende la luz.

25. Ud. es un científico importante.

26. Tú traduces documentos sobre la contabilidad.

3 Present system 2: Present subjunctive

3·1 *Since this book focuses on learning forms, it is safe to reveal that all the verbs in the first blank must be in the present indicative and all the verbs in the second blank must be in the present subjunctive. There are two challenges: identifying the subject in each case and then being aware of how to derive the right person and number according to the type of irregularities revealed in the first two principal parts.*

1. Nosotros no queremos que tú veas esa película.

2. Ellos dudan que ese político sea honesto.

3. Su papá le dice a su hijo que vaya a Europa a estudiar. *The present subjunctive of the verb **ir** is irregular to the point where it requires us to adjust the principal parts method by keeping in mind that the present indicative ends in a **y**—a fact that can help make it memorable.*

4. Yo no creo que los administradores sepan lo que hacen. *The present subjunctive of **saber** can be remembered more easily by remembering its relationship to **sapiens**, as in Homo Sapiens, or by thinking of turning the letter **b** upside down!*

5. Nosotros vamos al parque después de que mamá se despierte.

6. ¿Quiere tu papá que nosotros oigamos esa ópera? *The verb **oír** is an example of a consonant irregularity in the **yo** form—a type which is then repeated in all six forms of the present subjunctive.*

7. La mamá insiste en que sus hijos se pongan los zapatos.

8. Yo me alegro de que tú traduzcas cartas comerciales.

9. Los profesores se enfadan de que los alumnos no sepan la materia.

10. Juan, yo deseo que conozcas a mi vecino Tomás.

11. Señor Gómez, yo le ruego que no pierda el tiempo con esta propuesta. *Both of these verbs are good examples of **o → ue** and **e → ie** shoe pattern irregularities that are repeated in the stems of their present subjunctive forms.*

12. ¡Es inconcebible que la propuesta sea tan mal concebida!

13. Me da pena que tú te sientas mal hoy.

14. Yo le recomiendo al decano que vaya a Sur América.

15. ¡Es fantástico que tú puedas acompañarme esta noche!

16. Él busca una novia que merezca su amor.

17. Es necesario que los miembros del comité piensen mejor.

18. El cliente le pide al mesero que le traiga una copa de Merlot.

19. Yo tengo miedo de que mi papá se caiga en el jardín.

20. Juan tiene miedo de que su hijo vuele a Nueva York.

21. Ellas esperan que su hermana no se case con Juan.

22. Es magnífico que él no piense como el decano.

23. Yo te recomiendo que no pierdas tiempo hablando de esto.

24. Juan tiene miedo de que tú veas a su ex-novia.

25. Nosotros buscamos una secretaria que entienda bien las estadísticas.

26. Es increíble que ellos construyan un rascacielos en ese terreno.

27. ¿Quieres tú que yo esté aquí a las cuatro esta tarde?

28. Juan teme que los perros huyan al oír el disparo de la escopeta.

29. Es peligroso que los niños estén en la cocina. *The verb* **estar** *is irregular in the present subjunctive only in the sense of where the stress falls in the singular forms and in the third-person plural.*

30. Yo dudo que aquí haya nadie que traduzca esto al ruso.

3·2 *These dehydrated sentences are similar to those in the previous exercise: the first verb must be in the present indicative, and the second is found in the subordinated clause (introduced always by* **que***) and must be in the present subjunctive.*

1. Juan quiere que yo conduzca a la tienda.

2. Tú esperas que ella no vaya a la playa.

3. Es dudoso que ellos puedan cantar esta noche.

4. Es necesario que tú duermas antes de que vuelva tu padre.

5. Tú deseas que yo busque un libro que sea interesante.

6. Ellas insisten en que tú vengas a la fiesta temprano.

7. No hay nadie en el comité que sea capaz.

8. La gente tonta no cree que sea importante aprender lenguas.

9. ¿No crees tú que ella sea traidora?

10. Él insiste en que tú empieces la tarea pronto.

11. El dueño te busca para que le pagues el alquiler.

12. Yo te recomiendo que leas la novela.

13. Antes de que tú y yo tengamos clase mañana, es necesario que tú leas el artículo.

14. Me da pena que te duela la cabeza.

15. Juan quiere que ella encienda la luz.

16. Ellos me piden que yo les dé dinero.

17. Mi amigo insiste en que nosotros lleguemos temprano.

18. Yo tengo miedo de que mi hija conduzca el carro.

19. Nosotros esperamos que ella no traiga su perro a la fiesta.

20. Me molesta mucho que ellos pidan ese plato.

21. Me gusta que ella me dé un beso.

22. Yo espero que tú vengas a la fiesta mañana.

23. Tú y Juana no quieren que Juan esté en la misma clase.

24. Nosotros les decimos a Juan y Tomás que tengan cuidado.

25. Es fantástico que ellos conozcan a mi jefe esta noche.

26. Es importante que nosotros estemos en la reunión.

27. ¿Quieres tú que nosotros vengamos a las diez esta noche?

28. Mis padres no creen que yo tenga problemas económicos.

29. Juan le dice a su hijo que no vaya a las montañas mañana.

30. Nosotros buscamos una película que sea intrigante.

4 Present system 3: Imperatives

4·1   *When you need to find the command form of a verb, there are two things to remember. First, the affirmative **tú** and **vosotros** commands are the only ones that are not subjunctive in form. Second, there are no options about the placement of object pronouns. Affirmative commands must have them attached to the end of the command. For negative commands, they must be detached and placed between the word **no** and the appropriate (subjunctive) form.*

1. ¡Dáselos!

2. ¡Traígaselas!

3. ¡Venid a la fiesta!

4. ¡Sepan esto: él es honesto!

5. ¡Suélteme!

6. ¡No te caigas!

7. ¡Ponlos aquí!

8. ¡No coloquen la mesa aquí!

9. ¡No apaguéis la luz!

10. ¡Encuéntrenlo!

11. ¡Véla!

12. ¡No lo busques ahora!

13. ¡No tengas miedo! *or* ¡No lo tengas!

14. ¡Salgan!

15. ¡Empezadla!

16. ¡No quieras esto! *or* ¡No lo quieras! *Either **esto** or **lo** can be used when referring to an abstract idea, which in English is expressed as "that."*

17. ¡Págalas!

18. ¡No seas tonto! *or* ¡No seas tonta!

19. ¡Conduzca con cuidado!

20. ¡Tradúzcalo!

21. ¡Llegue temprano!

22. ¡No se sienten aquí!

23. ¡Piensen primero!

24. ¡No se sienta mal!

25. ¡Comiéncenla! *The group is not all composed of friends, hence the **Uds.** form.*

26. ¡Dámelas!

27. ¡Devuélvelos!

28. ¡No propongan esto! *or* ¡No lo propongan!

29. ¡No lo aprueben!

30. ¡No te mueras!

5   Infinitive system 1: Imperfect indicative

5·1   *When you know you need the imperfect indicative, remember that there are only three irregular verbs: **ver**, **ser**, and **ir**. Also, don't forget that the first- and third-persons singular are identical and that -**er** and -**ir** verbs share the same set of endings.*

1. Los chicos se ponían los pantalones cuando entró su mamá.

2. Simón Bolívar era un general importante en el Siglo XIX.

3. Como yo se lo decía a mi amigo...

4. En ese pueblo, las mujeres mandaban.

5. En la playa la semana pasada, yo veía muchas cosas interesantes.

6. ¿Dónde estabas tú ayer?

7. De niño, yo no podía cruzar las calles solo.

8. Nosotros íbamos a la tienda cuando se nos pinchó una llanta.

9. Nosotros manejábamos desde Xalapa cuando oímos la noticia sobre el terremoto.

10. Ella lo conocía muy bien cuando eran niños.

11. Pensé que perdía el juicio con toda la tarea que tenía.

12. Vosotros trabajabais en Málaga en aquel entonces, ¿no?

13. ¡Lo que me faltaba – perder la billetera!

14. A esos niños no les gustaba ese cuento de hadas.

15. Mientras Juan <u>se caía</u>, logró agarrar una raíz y se salvó.

16. Su mamá le <u>repetía</u> las mismas instrucciones a su hija cada día.

17. Hace 500 años, mucha gente <u>creía</u> en muchas supersticiones.

18. Cuando ella nos <u>servía</u> la limonada, se resbaló y se cayó.

19. ¿Cómo <u>se llamaba</u> tu bisabuelo?

20. Los atletas <u>volaban</u> a Chicago cuando empezó a nevar.

21. Cuando ellos eran niños, no <u>podían</u> hablar bien.

22. Mientras nosotros <u>veíamos</u> la película, mi mamá preparó las palomitas.

23. Nosotros <u>íbamos</u> a la escuela cuando vimos el accidente.

24. <u>Era</u> una noche de tormentas y teníamos mucho miedo.

25. Los alumnos no <u>entendían</u> nada de lo que decía el profesor.

26. Cuando yo <u>tenía</u> seis años, vivíamos en Texas.

27. Mientras ella <u>escuchaba</u> la radio, trabajaba.

28. Mientras Thomas Jefferson <u>se moría</u>, <u>se moría</u> también John Adams.

29. El jardín <u>crecía</u> más rápido el año pasado.

30. Da Vinci <u>creaba</u> muchas obras de arte mientras estudiaba ciencias.

5·2   *The biggest challenge in this exercise is recognizing the person and number of the verb forms. If this exercise was difficult for you, look up and write out the principal parts for each verb you missed.*

1. decías
2. trabajaba
3. conducía
4. veía
5. era
6. iba
7. veías
8. creías
9. querían
10. perdía
11. encontraba
12. pensaba
13. pensaba
14. rompía
15. era
16. iba
17. buscaba
18. dormía
19. comía
20. servías
21. leía
22. daba
23. veía
24. querían
25. salían
26. subíamos

6   Infinitive system 2: Future

6·1   *Aside from the three groups of irregular stems, the principal challenge with the simple future tense is remembering that there is one set of endings for all verbs and that those endings are added to the infinitive.*

1. Su mamá no <u>podrá</u> asistir a la reunión mañana.

2. ¿Qué <u>haremos</u> nosotros si se aprueba la propuesta? *The verb* **hacer** *is one of the two most irregular stems in the future—which simply means that its form cannot be predicted easily from its infinitive.*

3. Tú <u>verás</u> lo que vamos a hacer.

4. ¿Quién <u>querrá</u> venir a esta ciudad si no hay empleo? *Remember that the future stem of* **querer** *has two* **r***'s—it belongs to the group I call collapsed infinitives.*

5. Yo se lo <u>diré</u> luego. *The verb* **decir** *is the other of the two most irregular stems in the future— which simply means that its form cannot be predicted easily from its infinitive.*

6. ¿Dónde <u>estarán</u> María y Teresita? *Notice that* **estar** *is actually regular in the future.*

7. Ellos <u>se pondrán</u> las botas después de comer.

8. ¿Con quién <u>irás</u> tú a la playa este verano? *Another rare moment: the verb* **ir** *is regular in the future.*

9. Mis hermanos <u>conducirán</u> el camión hasta San Diego.

10. Ella no <u>querrá</u> salir con él nunca.

11. ¿<u>Habrá</u> alguien aquí que nos pueda ayudar a cambiar la llanta?

12. Creo que su bebé <u>se parecerá</u> a la mamá.

13. Si no cambia de opinión, esta mujer lo <u>sentirá</u>.

14. Mi papá <u>vendrá</u> en julio. *Remember that verbs whose stems end in an* **l** *or an* **n** *are what I've called the d-stem group of verbs whose future stem is irregular.*

15. Igual que tú, yo <u>podré</u> ir al baile este fin de semana. *Note that* **poder** *is not a d-stem verb but rather a collapsed infinitive because its stem actually ends in* **d***.*

16. Como siempre, Carlos me <u>pedirá</u> los apuntes de clase.

17. Héctor <u>saldrá</u> temprano del trabajo hoy.

18. El mesero dice que Juan no <u>pedirá</u> la torta de manzana.

19. Las chicas que están patinando sobre el hielo <u>se caerán</u>.

20. Lorena dice que pronto <u>volará</u> a Chicago.

21. Emilio <u>tendrá</u> problemas en sus exámenes si no estudia más.

22. ¡Tarde o temprano, todos <u>sabrán</u> que tienes la culpa por cobarde!

23. Raúl <u>pondrá</u> todo en orden antes de salir.

24. A mi ver, esto no <u>podrá</u> ser resuelto sin costarle algo.

25. Ipólito no <u>entenderá</u> el plan.

26. Dos chicos <u>pasarán</u> por la tienda a solicitar fondos para una obra caritativa.

27. Oficialmente, <u>será</u> primavera después del equinoccio de marzo.

28. Roberto <u>verá</u> la gloria que merece, un día.

29. Al morir, dicen algunos, todos nosotros <u>sabremos</u> la verdad.

30. ¡Ella pronto <u>se parecerá</u> a la otra si sigue viéndola tan a menudo!

6·2

1. Juan y Carlos tendrán una semana libre pronto.

2. Yo pondré los libros en el estante esta tarde.

3. Teresa y Juana no dirán la verdad.

4. ¿Saldrás tú inmediatamente después del concierto?

5. Yo querré hablar con Rosa este fin de semana.

6. ¿Quién podrá esquiar mañana?

7. ¿Verán Uds. esta película conmigo?

8. Ella hablará contigo mañana.

9. Nosotros miraremos el programa luego.

10. Mi padre saldrá cuando se recupere.

11. ¿Quién me dará un regalo en la fiesta?

12. Esto no cabrá en este cajón.

13. ¿A quién le mandarás estos libros?

14. ¿Qué hará el decano?

15. Su madre le repetirá las instrucciones.

16. Yo no le serviré nada.

17. Tú irás a Europa el año que viene.

18. ¿Uds. se lo pedirán a Juana?

19. Yo la amaré siempre.

20. Ud. vivirá en Costa Rica en diez años.

21. ¿Qué dirán los vecinos?

22. ¿Qué comerás tú esta noche?

23. Esta propuesta creará problemas.

24. Una nueva cadena de montañas se formará.

25. ¿Quién lo creerá?

26. Mi mamá no me lo dará nunca.

27. Yo se la escribiré luego.

28. Tú se lo leerás al niño.

29. Juan lo tendrá, probablemente.

30. ¿Quién estará en la puerta?

7 Infinitive system 3: Conditional

7·1   *The verbs with irregular stems are the same ones that were irregular in the future—and in exactly the same way. Most errors in the conditional are due to the fact that the endings are identical to the endings for -er and -ir verbs in the imperfect indicative. Remember, though, that in the conditional these endings are added to the infinitive or irregular stem. Besides providing exercise with the forms of the conditional, this exercise also reinforces the fact that the conditional is used with the imperfect subjunctive to show what "would" happen if something else were so. Likewise, the conditional perfect, formed with the conditional of* **haber** *+ the invariable participle, shows what "would have" happened if something had been so.*

1. ¿Qué harías tú en mi lugar?

2. Si fueras al norte de Alaska, ¿qué verías?

3. Para ganar dinero con este plan, nosotros tendríamos que invertir demasiado.

4. Juana querría invitarlo a la fiesta, pero es que Carlos querría sacarla a bailar.

5. Si ellos fueran honestos, dirían la verdad.

6. El Congreso declararía la guerra contra cualquier país que nos atacara.

7. Si hiciera calor, yo no me pondría el suéter.

8. Si tú tuvieras veintiún años, podrías acompañarme al bar.

9. Si el comité entendiera algo sobre las Artes, sabría que su plan es tonto.

10. Yo no iría a esa ciudad nunca, aun si me pagaran el vuelo y el hotel.

11. Me gustaría comer en ese restaurante, pero no tengo suficiente tiempo.

12. ¿Crees tú que habría paz en el mundo si nadie estuviera muriendo de hambre?

13. Ella se sentaría en el parque si no fuera de noche.

14. En caso de incendio, claro, nosotros saldríamos inmediatamente.

15. ¿En qué pensarían los Fundadores en 1776?

16. Con una inversión tan grande, ellos recibirían muchos dividendos.

17. Ellas saben que Juan está aquí, porque de lo contrario, vendrían a nuestra fiesta.

18. Sin empleo, ¿cómo crees que nosotros pagaríamos las cuentas?

19. Creo que valdría la pena ir de excursión a las Pirámides de Egipto.

20. Si ella fuera mi novia, yo la esperaría con paciencia.

21. ¿Qué buscaría Juan Ponce de León? – Ah, ¡la Fuente de la Juventud!

22. Si ellos jugaran contra los Yankees, perderían sin duda.

23. A ver, ¿los vikingos sabrían algo sobre la navegación en el hemisferio del sur?

24. Si de veras hubiera vivido en Seattle, él conocería Pike's Market mejor.

25. Juan y Teresa entenderían la lección si hubieran asistido a clase esta semana.

26. Si yo buscara en mi cuarto, encontraría mi billetera.

27. En el planeta Marte, ¿cree que oiríamos nuestra estación de radio favorita?

28. Con una dosis tan fuerte, hasta se moriría un caballo.

29. Con tan poco que perder y tanto que ganar, ellos volverían a invertir su dinero.

30. Si ellos realmente tuvieran un plan, empezarían a ponerlo por obra.

7·2 *Most of the items in this exercise contain an implicit if clause. Questions 16 and 18, however, require students to provide the proper form of the imperfect subjunctive.*

1. Yo no iría a ese lugar porque es peligroso.

2. Tú y Carlos saldrían en caso de emergencia.

3. ¿Ellos sabrían la verdad en ese momento?

4. Con tanta lluvia, ellos se pondrían los impermeables.

5. En tu lugar, yo iría a la fiesta.

6. Juan vendría, pero no puede.

7. Ella querría un vaso de agua.

8. Si fueran honestos, ellos dirían la verdad.

9. En una granja, yo tendría que ordeñar las vacas.

10. Juan tendría cinco años en 1969.

11. Yo podría hacerlo, pero no hay tiempo.

12. Habría una guerra en caso de un ataque.

13. Hace buen tiempo, pero si no, ellas saldrían.

14. Ellos podrían ayudarme mañana.

15. A ella le gustaría tomar un refresco.

16. Tú vendrías a la fiesta si tuvieras tiempo.

17. Ellos comprarían ropa con una tarjeta de crédito.

18. Él se pondría una corbata si fuera una ocasión formal.

19. ¿Qué harías tú en su lugar?

20. Yo no le diría mentiras a mi papá.

21. ¿Qué pensaría Ud. en mi lugar?

22. No valdría la pena subir la montaña.

23. Ella haría su vestido, pero no tiene tiempo.

24. Me gustaría pasar más tiempo con mi hija.

25. ¿Viajarías tú a Antártida?

26. Los chicos harían el viaje, pero no lo permiten sus padres.

27. Ella se pondría los zapatos si hiciera frío.

28. Yo no podría hacerlo ni por todo el oro del mundo.

29. Uds. saldrían, pero hay que trabajar.

30. Nosotros iríamos a Roma si el vuelo no costara tanto.

8 Preterit system 1: Preterit indicative

8·1
1. Juan corrió a la estación, pero no <u>pudo</u> llegar a tiempo.

2. Ellos <u>fueron</u> al parque por dos horas.

3. Yo no le <u>dije</u> nada ayer.

4. ¿<u>Quisiste</u> tú hacer la tarea?

5. El ladrón <u>huyó</u> cuando oyó el gatillo.

6. ¿Dónde <u>estuviste</u> tú ayer a las tres?

7. Yo me puse el sombrero y salí en seguida.

8. Julio César fue dictador del Imperio Romano.

9. Ellos condujeron por cinco horas sin parar.

10. Nosotros sólo lo supimos a la última hora.

11. Se dice que «Puchacay» es el lugar donde el diablo perdió su sombrero.

12. El fantasma apareció enfrente de la chimenea.

13. Al oír esto, Elena se sintió muy triste. *Remember that the verbs that have a single-vowel stem change in the present exhibit this change in the preterit only in their third-person forms.*

14. Los niños estaban tan cansados que se durmieron en seguida.

15. Yo se lo pagué ayer y en efectivo.

16. Juan pidió la mano de Teresa anoche. *Remember that the verbs that have a single-vowel stem change in the present exhibit this change in the preterit only in their third-person forms.*

17. Cuando me lo contó, yo pensé que estaba loco.

18. Las meseras me sirvieron mucho café esta mañana. *Remember that the verbs that have a single-vowel stem change in the present exhibit this change in the preterit only in their third-person forms.*

19. Los alpinistas se cayeron 10 metros antes de recuperarse.

20. Yo te busqué por una hora.

21. Juan no trajo traje, así que no nadó.

22. Nosotros les dijimos todos los detalles en la reunión ayer.

23. Yo estuve en la biblioteca esperándote a las cuatro.

24. ¿Pudiste tú arreglar la motocicleta?

25. Su mamá le repitió dos veces lo que ella quería. *Remember that the verbs that have a single-vowel stem change in the present exhibit this change in the preterit only in their third-person forms.*

26. Yo no hice la tarea porque no me sentía bien.

27. De repente, ellos oyeron un grito.

28. Yo te vi en la calle.

29. Yo te lo di ayer. *One way to remember the forms of **dar** in the preterit is to imagine that it is pretending to be an -**ir** verb. Another way is to remember that the forms of **dar** and **ver** rhyme in the preterit.*

30. ¿Cuándo lo supiste tú?

8·2

1. Yo no tuve tiempo la semana pasada.

2. Ese señor nos dijo la verdad.

3. Yo no te vi por dos días.

4. Ellos trajeron los libros a la biblioteca. *Remember that verbs whose preterit stem ends in -**j** drop the **i** of the ending in the third-person plural: "**J** isn't followed by **I**."*

5. Ellas quisieron llamarme una vez.

6. Él anduvo de un lado al otro de la ciudad.

7. ¿Quién me dio este regalo?

8. ¡Yo no lo hice!

9. La niña se puso la falda antes de salir anoche.

10. Ellos pudieron escalar la montaña después de cuatro días.

11. La maestra definió la palabra en clase ayer.

12. Yo se lo dije en las barbas.

13. Juana me escribió una carta de amor.

14. Ella lo supo por teléfono.

15. Él empezó a reír.

16. Los conejos huyeron de los perros.

17. ¿Para qué le sirvió a Juan estudiar tanto?

18. Yo te conocí hace dos años.

19. ¿Quién tradujo estas cartas?

20. Ella me pidió un beso.

21. Los obreros construyeron el puente.

22. Yo le pagué lo que le debía.

23. Ella durmió diez horas. *Remember that in the preterit **dormir** and **morir** show an o → u stem change in their third-person forms only.*

24. El profesor salió de la clase a las tres de la tarde.

25. Nosotros trabajamos por una semana.

26. Yo vine a Seattle en 2001.

27. Uds. le repitieron las instrucciones.

28. Ud. se puso triste al escuchar las noticias.

29. Tú estuviste esperando a las dos.

30. Yo no te busqué hasta las tres.

9 Preterit system 2: Imperfect subjunctive

9·1 *All difficulties in forming the imperfect subjunctive are due to not knowing the preterit for both regular and irregular verbs. This exercise contains examples of all the situations in which the subjunctive must be used—and, here at least, the imperfect subjunctive is always in the second blank.*

1. Su mamá le dijo que dijera la verdad siempre.

2. Nosotros buscábamos un artesano que hiciera figuras de madera.

3. Yo te dije que tuvieras cuidado.

4. Ud. <u>esperaba</u> que ella te <u>quisiera</u>. *The preterit of **esperar** is less likely since the meaning of the verb has to do with a state of mind.*

5. Ellas <u>insistieron</u> en que él <u>fuera</u> despedido.

6. Tú <u>dudaste/dudabas</u> que él <u>anduviera</u> tanto tiempo en la nieve sin zapatos. *The preterit of **dudar** would be used if the speaker wished to show a reaction, while the imperfect would indicate a state of mind.*

7. Tú me <u>recomendaste</u> que <u>me pusiera</u> un abrigo.

8. ¡<u>Era/Fue</u> magnífico que tú <u>fueras</u> a Madrid para estudiar! *Logically, even the present of **ser** (es) is permissible in the first blank.*

9. Yo <u>me alegraba/alegré</u> de que Juana y Teresa <u>pudieran</u> venir a mi fiesta.

10. Ella no <u>creyó/creía</u> que su novio <u>supiera</u> que le había engañado con Pedro.

11. Yo <u>esperaba</u> que tú no <u>perdieras</u> la carrera de los 400 metros.

12. Nos <u>gustó/gustaba</u> que ella <u>se pareciera</u> a una actriz famosa.

13. Ella <u>prefería/prefirió</u> que ellos no <u>vinieran</u> a su casa con el perro. *Remember that the third-person preterit of **preferir** has a vowel change of e → i.*

14. Tú <u>querías</u> que los niños <u>se sentaran</u> en una mesa aparte.

15. El médico me <u>aconsejó</u> que <u>durmiera</u> ocho horas todas las noches. *Remember that since the imperfect subjunctive is formed from the third-person plural of the preterit, any irregularity found there will appear in all six forms of the imperfect subjunctive. In this case, the o → u stem vowel change of **dormir** appears in the **yo** form of the imperfect subjunctive.*

16. Ella <u>quería</u> que su novio <u>pidiera</u> su mano en el restaurante. *Here, the vowel stem change of e → i appears in the imperfect subjunctive, since the third-person plural of **pedir** is **pidieron**.*

17. En ese momento, yo <u>dudé</u> que ella <u>pensara</u> en nuestro bien.

18. Ella me <u>dijo</u> que no les <u>sirviera</u> el chocolate a los niños.

19. Juan <u>tuvo/tenía</u> miedo de que su perro <u>se cayera</u> al río.

20. Mi papá siempre <u>prefería</u> que nosotros <u>voláramos</u> a Europa. *Note that the **nosotros** forms of the imperfect subjunctive are stressed on the first a of the ending.*

21. La maestra <u>insistió/insistía</u> en que los niños no <u>jugaran</u> en clase.

22. ¡<u>Fue</u> fantástico que tú <u>tocaras</u> el piano anoche!

23. Yo <u>buscaba/busqué</u> un mecánico que <u>supiera</u> arreglar mi coche.

24. Ellos <u>dudaban/dudaron</u> que <u>llovieva</u>.

25. La compañía <u>buscó/buscaba</u> una secretaria que <u>entendiera</u> chino y árabe.

26. El presidente <u>mandó</u> que <u>se construyera</u> una base militar allí.

27. Me <u>dio</u> pena que tú <u>oyeras</u> esto de tu propio amigo.

28. Ellos <u>se entristecieron</u> de que ese actor <u>se muriera</u> en ese momento.

29. El cocinero nos <u>recomendó</u> que <u>hirviéramos</u> la sopa por 20 minutos. *The verb **hervir** has an e → i stem change in the third person of the preterit.*

30. Te <u>dije</u> ayer que <u>tradujeras</u> esta carta urgente.

9·2 *After simply not knowing the forms, the most likely error when constructing sentences in this exercise is the omission of **que** to link main and subordinate clauses.*

1. Si ella se casara con Juan, no tendrían hijos por cinco años.
2. Tú insististe ayer en que yo hiciera una torta.
3. Si nosotros fuéramos a Chicago, tendríamos frío.
4. Ella dudó/dudaba que tú y yo fuéramos novios.
5. Ellas no se alegraban de que yo recibiera un ascenso.
6. Yo me bañé antes de que tú vinieras a mi casa.
7. Mi hermana esperaba que yo la llamara anoche.
8. Si ella volviera a pedir, yo aceptaría la oferta.
9. Juan lo explicó para que ellos lo entendieran.
10. Nosotros decidimos salir, con tal de que Teresa viniera también.
11. Ella se puso el suéter en caso de que hiciera frío.
12. Si tú vinieras, nos divertiríamos mucho más.
13. Ellos practicaron para que tú escucharas un buen concierto.
14. Ella me recomendó que visitara el Museo del Vaticano.
15. Su mamá insistió/insistía en que su hijo se vistiera solo.
16. Tú buscabas/buscaste un fotógrafo que pudiera filmar el/un partido de baloncesto.
17. Nosotros queríamos que tú pusieras la mesa.
18. Ella insistió en que sus amigos no hicieran ruidos en la fiesta.
19. Mi amigo prefirió que tú y yo no conociéramos a su hermana. *Remember the accent placement for the **nosotros** form of the imperfect subjunctive.*
20. Yo esperaba que tú no me esperaras.
21. Si tú fueras a Europa, verías museos famosos.
22. Los astronautas temían que aparecieran unos extraterrestres.
23. Ellos dudaban que hubiera vida en otros planetas.
24. Ella buscó/buscaba una amiga que trajera el pastel.
25. Jaime necesitaba/necesitó una computadora que pudiera tocar música.
26. Yo no quería que ella se pusiera ese vestido.
27. No me agradó que ella traicionara a sus colegas.
28. Ayer no había nadie aquí que supiera pilotar un avión.
29. El profesor quería que los alumnos tomaran su clase de poesía.
30. Si yo tuviera suerte, ganaría la lotería.

10 Participial system 1: Gerunds

10·1 *The most likely difficulty when doing this exercise is not knowing the irregular form of the helping verb—the first one in the parentheses, such as **iba** (**ir**). Other difficulties include the handful of gerunds with single-vowel changes, such as **durmiendo**, **diciendo**, or **sirviendo**, and the **i → y** spelling change when **i** falls between vowels, such as **leyendo** (**leer**).*

1. Ayer, mi amigo <u>iba hablando</u> consigo mismo mientras caminaba.

2. Aún después de estudiar el cálculo, <u>seguirá siendo</u> difícil por un rato.

3. ¿No entiendes lo que yo te <u>estoy diciendo</u>?

4. Aún después de que ella lo abandonó, él la <u>siguió queriendo</u>.

5. ¡No entres! Yo <u>estoy vistiéndome/me estoy vistiendo</u>.

6. Su papá entró en el cuarto cuando sus hijos <u>estaban poniéndose/se estaban poniendo</u> las botas.

7. Vi que mi novia <u>iba cantando</u> mientras se bañaba.

8. El único vuelo que sale mañana <u>estará volando</u> a Tegucigalpa.

9. Hijo, sabes cuánto me molesta tener que <u>estar repitiéndote</u> todo.

10. El jefe se fue, y nosotros <u>nos quedamos trabajando</u>.

11. ¡Uf! Este partido es una pérdida de tiempo: ese equipo <u>irá perdiendo</u> toda la tarde.

12. Cuando la maestra los dejó solos, los chicos <u>continuaron</u> jugando.

13. Ay, amiga, no quiero que tú <u>estés sintiéndote/te estés sinitiendo</u> mal por culpa de él.

14. El pintor no quería que nosotros <u>estuviéramos hablando</u> cerca de su lugar de trabajo.

15. Ella es tan bella que no puedo creer lo que yo <u>estoy viendo</u>.

16. Me molestó que ellas nos <u>siguieran pidiendo</u> el mismo favor.

17. La Bella Durmiente del Bosque <u>se quedó durmiendo</u> por 100 años.

18. Veo que en este restaurante los meseros ya <u>están sirviendo</u> la cena.

19. No pudo abrir el paracaídas, así que <u>siguió cayendo</u> hasta dar con la tierra.

20. Cuando yo oí el disparo, yo <u>me fui volando</u> para no estar en la calle.

21. Ya veo que ese niño <u>está teniendo</u> problemas en la escuela.

22. Lentamente, todos <u>estaban enfermándose/se estaban enfermando</u> debido a un derrame de gas tóxico.

23. Su papá fue un ignorante: no quería que su hijo <u>se quedara leyendo</u> todo el tiempo.

24. A pesar de pruebas, hay gente que <u>sigue creyendo</u> en supersticiones.

25. Cuando su abuelo <u>estaba muriéndose/se estaba muriendo</u>, él vivía en otro país.

26. Muy pronto nosotros <u>estaremos construyendo</u> una regadera en la Logia.

27. Después del incendio, Juan <u>siguió oyendo</u> las sirenas por una hora.

28. ¿Por qué me despertaste? ¿No viste que yo <u>estaba durmiendo</u>?

29. Se nos olvidó la olla y <u>continuó hirviendo</u> hasta evaporarse toda el agua.

30. A lo mejor, esta noche ella <u>estará traduciendo</u> otros documentos importantes.

11   Participial system 2: The seven perfect tenses

11·1   *This exercise challenges students' ability to use the whole range of perfect tenses, indicative and subjunctive. Yet the challenge can be cut down to size by remembering that (1) there are only seven tenses of the helping verb **haber**; (2) the past (or passive) participle is invariable; and (3) there are only a handful of irregular past participles.*

1. Es dudoso que ellos <u>hayan dicho</u> la verdad hasta ahora.

2. La editorial <u>habría impreso</u> el libro si el editor no hubiera creído que era mentira.

3. Yo <u>he cubierto</u> la olla para que no se enfríe la sopa.

4. Si esa compañía te hubiera contratado, <u>habrías vivido</u> en Puerto Rico por dos años ya.

5. Me pregunto si tu hermana <u>ha vuelto</u> ya del Perú.

6. Habrías ganado mucho más dinero si <u>hubieras hecho</u> algo con la tecnología.

7. Habríamos podido vender este modelo si <u>hubiéramos abierto</u> la tienda antes de las ocho.

8. Busco una novia que <u>haya ido</u> alguna vez a México.

9. Fui a la oficina con prisa, pero supe que ellos <u>habían resuelto</u> el problema.

10. Se me arruinó el reloj porque lo <u>había puesto</u> donde luego se cayó en el lavabo.

11. Me alegro de que ellos <u>hayan visto</u> la película recientemente.

12. Antes de que termine la guerra, muchos <u>habrán escrito</u> sus memorias.

13. El tanque <u>se habría roto</u> si lo hubiéramos levantado sin ti.

14. Esperamos ir a ver a nuestro bisabuelo con tal de que no <u>se haya muerto</u>.

15. ¿Qué <u>habrías hecho</u> tú con la vida si no te hubieras casado conmigo?

16. Ella habría tenido un problema con el jefe si <u>hubiera impreso</u> la carta.

17. Cuando me levanté esta mañana, vi que tú <u>habías vuelto</u> de las vacaciones.

18. Cuando ella esté de nuevo en casa luego, <u>habrá sabido</u> sobre el accidente.

19. Yo sé que María <u>ha puesto</u> la ropa en la secadora porque puedo oír el motor.

20. Cuando todos llegaron al hospital, su bisabuelo ya <u>había muerto</u>.

21. Para las cinco mañana, tú ya <u>habrás dicho</u> todo lo que se necesita decir.

22. Tuve que esperar esta mañana, porque el gerente todavía no <u>había abierto</u> la tienda.

23. Avísenos cuando ya <u>haya puesto</u> la mesa porque tenemos hambre.

24. Se pegó la sopa en la olla; la <u>habría cubierto</u> si hubiera sabido que pudiera pasar esto.

25. ¡Oye, pero <u>has roto</u> mi bicicleta, amigo!

26. Si yo no <u>hubiera escrito</u> ese mensaje, habríamos tenido que seguir su plan ridículo.

27. Espero que cuando yo llegue esta tarde, ella <u>habrá resuelto</u> la dificultad con Carlos.

28. Si ella <u>hubiera dicho</u> algo para revelar que el plan era ridículo, yo la habría respetado.

29. ¿Has visto tú un eclipse del sol alguna vez?

30. Cuando te gradúes, ya habrás hecho mucho para prepararte para tu carrera.

12 Participial system 3: Passive participles

12·1   *Remember that when constructing a passive voice sentence, the passive participle must agree with the noun it refers to in gender and number.*

1. La tienda fue abierta por el gerente a las nueve. *Since **abierta** refers to **tienda**, it must be feminine and singular.*

2. Los muebles son hechos por el carpintero. *Since **hechos** refers to **muebles**, it must be masculine and plural.*

3. Un barco de vela fue visto por nosotros.

4. Unas cartas serán escritas por mí.

5. Unas tortas fueron hechas por mi hermana.

6. El paquete ha sido puesto en la mesa por ti.

7. Los problemas son resueltos por nosotros todos los días.

8. Las macetas de flores fueron cubiertas por su madre.

9. La verdad será dicha por ella.

10. Dudo que la computadora haya sido puesto en la oficina por ellos.

11. Los juguetes serán rotos por ese chico.

12. Ojalá los artículos que necesito hayan sido impresos por ti.

12·2   *Remember that the passive voice is used much less in Spanish than in English, and thus, without further context, most of these sentences would sound a bit stilted in Spanish.*

1. Los paquetes han sido recibidos por Juan. *This is an example of the passive voice in the present perfect. In the present, one would say **Los paquetes son recibidos por Juan** ("The packages are received by John").*

2. El carro será arreglado por su hermano.

3. Las almohadas fueron hechas por mi abuela.

4. Las cartas fueron escritas por nosotros.

5. La bicicleta fue rota por él.

6. Los regalos serán abiertos por los niños.

7. La película fue vista por todos.

8. La verdad ha sido dicha por ella.

9. La tienda fue cerrada por el Sr. Gómez.

10. La casa fue vendida por la Sra. Reyes.

11. La comida fue preparada por nuestros amigos.

12. El cuarto de baño fue limpiado por el Sr. Ramírez.